BANTAM KNOWLEDGE THROUGH COLOR

WITCHCRAFT AND BLACK MAGIC

BY PETER HAINING

ILLUSTRATED BY JAN PARKER

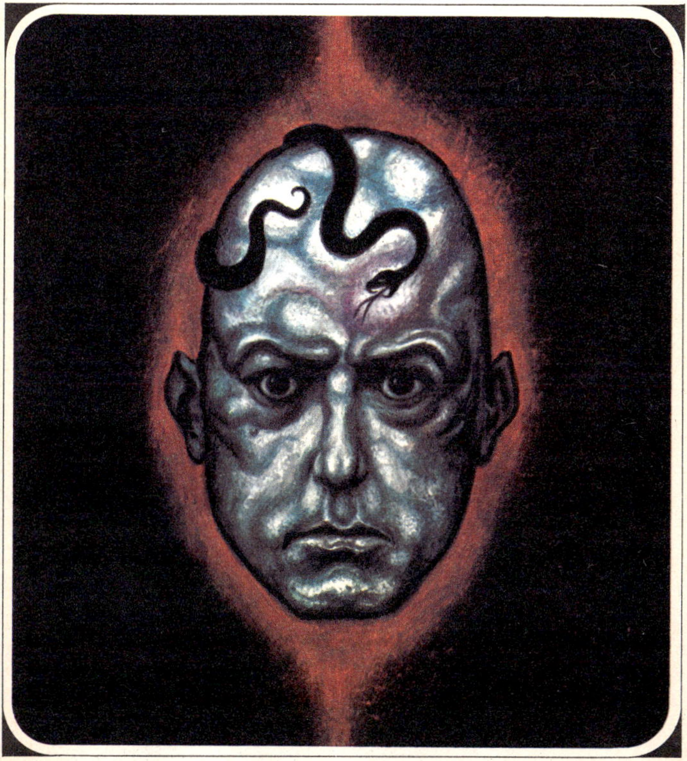

BANTAM BOOKS
TORONTO NEW YORK LONDON

FOREWORD

Much of witchcraft's fascination lies in its sinister association with the death-dealing rites and sexual excesses practiced in the name of Black Magic. But it has always included not only the "black" but also the "white." Witchcraft dates back to man's earliest attempts to relate himself to the scheme of his environment. Starting as a nature and fertility religion administered by the matriarchal element in prehistoric societies, witchcraft continued as a powerful force throughout history and is presently experiencing a real revival.

The reader learns about witchcraft's many facets: charms and potions, divination and clairvoyance, levitation, possession, the coven and the sabbat, familiars, werewolves, vampires and the rites of the Black Mass.

WITCHCRAFT AND BLACK MAGIC

A Bantam Book/published by arrangement with Grosset & Dunlap, Inc.

PRINTING HISTORY
Grosset & Dunlap All-Color Guide hardcover edition published March 1972
Bantam edition published April 1973
3rd printing

For Information address: Grosset & Dunlap, Inc., 51 Madison Ave., New York, N. Y. 10010.

Published simultaneously in the United States and Canada.

Bantam Books are published by Bantam Books, Inc. Its trademark, consisting of the words "Bantam Books" and the portrayal of a bantam, is registered in the United States Patent Office and in other countries. Marca Registrada. Bantam Books, Inc., 666 Fifth Avenue, New York, New York 10019.

PRINTED IN THE UNITED STATES OF AMERICA

CONTENTS

The traditional idea of the witch, complete with pointed hat, broomstick and imps. The truth, however, was somewhat different.

THE HISTORY OF WITCHCRAFT TO 1736

The origins of witchcraft

The word 'witchcraft' is one of the most widely used in modern occult language. With constant reference to the subject in all the media of communication, the word has come to have many meanings and many interpretations. In this study we shall endeavor to uncover not only the truth about witchcraft but also its beginnings, growth and place in society through the centuries of human existence. It is a huge picture and one which covers a vast canvas of people, places and times. Unfortunately we shall not be able to deal with every aspect as closely as we should like, but if the basic facts can be recounted the interested reader may pursue his search for further knowledge in the more scholarly volumes that are easily available.

Witchcraft, let it be said immediately, is still alive and

flourishing today, despite a terrifying history of bloodshed, persecution and misunderstanding. It is not greatly changed from its earliest beginnings in terms of underlying beliefs. And the rituals are not much changed either. But more of this later.

The word 'witch' derives from the Anglo-Saxon *wicca,* 'a magician who weakens the power of evil.' In his *Discourse on the Art of Witchcraft* (1610), Thomas Pickering defined the practitioners a little more closely when he said: 'He or she cannot hurt, torment, curse or kill, but onely heale and cure the hurt inflicted upon men.' Dr. Gerald Gardner, the most famous self-confessed witch of this century, has written further: 'There have been witches in all ages and countries. That is, there have been men and women who have had a knowledge of cures, philters, charms and love potions and at times poisons. Sometimes it is believed they could affect the weather, bringing rain or drought. At times they were hated, at times they were loved; at times they were

Over the centuries we find the real witchcraft has not changed much. Here, for instance, modern witches adore the Old Gods . . .

highly honored, at times persecuted. They claimed to be, or were credited with being, in communication with the world of spirits, the dead, and sometimes with the lesser gods.'

The origins of witchcraft lie buried in prehistory. Archeologists tell us that in prehistoric human groups the woman held a position of prominence. The woman's role in birth, her sexual cycle which coincided with that of the moon, and her role in the gathering of plants and herbs laid the groundwork for her later preeminence in witchcraft. She acted as counselor of wisdom and priestess to the gods of nature. It was her responsibility to see that these deities were placated so that man would secure good hunting and fishing, and there would be many children and increase in the herds to keep the tribe strong. The man's responsibilities were, by necessity, far more direct at this time: the providing of food, shelter and defense against attack.

Because of her position, woman was free to experiment:

. . . while turning back to the dawn of time we see primitive man and woman worshiping the Horned God and the Great Mother.

her mind could dwell not only on ways to grow better crops and cure sickness but also on what lay outside the boundaries of material existence. Her mind began to turn to the metaphysical. Women discussed the world around them: the light and darkness, the driving rain and rushing waters, the changing seasons and the mystery of birth and death. And what more natural conclusion should they have come to than that, apart from the helpful gods, there must also be those of evil and danger?

From such basic conjecture came religion: a religion shaped and developed by woman who was, naturally, its first priestess. Her knowledge of herbs provided her with the power to heal; her pondering on the mysteries with the ability to command — if necessary, by fear. She was, in fact, 'doctor' and priestess. To give direction to her religion, she named her gods, each governing an area of existence and each to receive its special tributes.

Predominant above all was the goddess of fertility, the Great Mother, for the life force was at the center of existence and its importance was indisputable to the primitive mind. Her symbol was the Moon, and she is usually represented as

having three faces: the Maid, the Mother and the Wise Ancient—the New Moon, the Full Moon and the Waning Moon. Each lunar period was celebrated and the men would join with the women in adoration of the Great Mother—concluding the festivities with a sexual ritual which had the by-product of ensuring the continuation of the tribe!

It was not long, of course, before the male element created its own gods, the most important of these being the Hunting God, who presided over the animals that were so vital to the group's existence. For reasons now almost impossible to define accurately, the Hunting God—represented as a figure with horns—became the most important of all the deities, looking after not only man's well-being on earth but also his passage through the dark world of death. Later, even more typically male-oriented religious developments centered around gods of the sun, thunder and lightning. The Great Mother, however, always retained her hold, frequently returning to influence as the spouse of a sun god.

But men never completely replaced the women as priests or oracles. Since birth and death were not only mysterious but so often linked, and primitive humans so helpless in influencing either, men feared what women accepted as natural. The patterns of belief mirrored what each believed, the male gods often proclaiming sex and menstruating women ritually unclean. And, because the unknown is hated and feared at the same time, women were often suspect and suffered much more severely under witchcraft persecutions.

The practice of witchcraft, either by individual or group, was to last down the centuries—but not for long was it to escape misunderstanding, once the first great civilizations had begun to introduce more sophisticated religions.

The rise of witch magic

The practice of what we now define as witchcraft developed primarily in western, central and northern Europe; it was

The Great Mother, the goddess of life and fertility, as envisaged by the ancient peoples. Each face represents a phase of the moon.

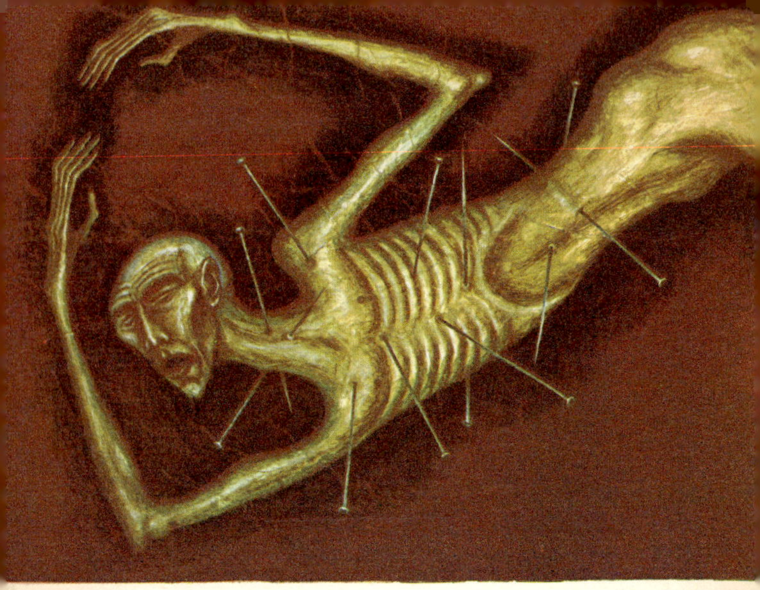

The powers of witchcraft were extremely varied, embracing sickness, health, and even death through the use of a victim's effigy.

particularly suited to the cold, dark and wet climate of this part of the world. (In the warmer regions of the south, other rituals were developing that contained elements similar to witchcraft, but here we are concentrating on the origin and spread of what can best be termed European witchcraft.)

As we have seen, in prehistoric times man's needs were simple, but as his intelligence developed he began to ponder on the power of ritual magic and saw that it could have two purposes—good or evil, 'white' magic or 'black' magic. (At this stage we should think of 'white' magic as being creative and for the benefit of life, whereas 'black' magic signifies the destructive element, devoted to causing sickness and death.)

Man's herd instinct was now well developed and, as one group began to war on another, the work of the witch-priests was often directed against the enemy. They began to evolve spells and rituals to gain victory for their people in these

confrontations—mostly using the simple formula that if one imitated a person in effigy and then destroyed the likeness, the victim would meet the same fate. Because of this, primitive man had to guard carefully against losing his hair, nails or items of clothing which an enemy might secure and use in a 'black' magic ritual.

The witch-priest's ability to perform this and other forms of magic gave him, of course, an honored position in his tribe—and far-ranging powers. He chose the method of attacking an enemy and the time to begin; he divined the future for his people from the stars and the entrails of animals; and he healed sickness with his special brews and potions. But skill in bringing down vengeance or death on the enemy was the criterion by which he was judged and valued. He also played a part in seeing the ghosts of the dead consigned to the 'other world beyond the sky'—casting his special magic over the corpse to ensure the spirit did not return to haunt the people. In these times there was almost nothing that was believed to be beyond the powers of the witch, and his magic controlled every aspect of people's lives.

The power of suggestion and dance

To keep their hold over the people, the witch-priests developed the paraphernalia of mystery around their craft. They created special clothes and masks (often the preserved heads of animals), devised ritual dances at which power for good or evil was conjured and discovered the ability to do with their bodies as they chose.

They could withstand considerable pain—thrusting their limbs into fire—and allegedly had the ability to rise into the air and fly. It was said, too, that they possessed the secret of changing their shape from man to beast and back again. Most of these abilities were doubtless due to their knowledge of the effects of autosuggestion on unquestioning and fearful minds and to their own acting talent, a necessary part of the early witch's equipment.

These magicians were also aware of the very real power of the dance and the ritual ceremony. Four times a year, at the period when the seasons changed, the worshipers were gathered together to pay homage to the gods for the fertility of the fields, rivers, livestock and womenfolk. The times of these rites were May Eve, marking the coming of spring, Lammas, in honor of incoming summer, Halloween or All Hallow's Eve, denoting autumn, and Candlemas for winter.

They were great occasions for letting off pent-up energy and, of course, sexual promiscuity was rife. However, one should remember in this context that early peoples did not look upon sexual intercourse from the same moral standpoint as we do today. Their indiscriminate couplings were not sinful but one of their few forms of expression, used to show the Great Mother how they appreciated her gift of union between man and woman.

At these gatherings were seen the broomsticks which have become so much a part of the mythology of witchcraft. In fact, the broomstick had a symbolic role, representing domestic order and well-being, and was brought to the meetings by the women. As they approached, they would sit astride their brooms and mimic horsemen riding into an assembly

The belief that witches could fly appeared early in witchcraft's mythology. They were said to travel to the Sabbat by broomstick.

before their leader. Hence the origin of the stories of witches flying.

We know that at some of these meetings an occasional blood sacrifice of an animal was made to the gods. Indeed it was stories of these ritual killings that early opponents of the craft were to embroider and enlarge into tales of human sacrifices to the Devil.

While the great majority of these ceremonies were directed to worship of the gods of fertility and hunting and their associates, there were others led by the more curious (and probably evil) magicians that strayed along the path of dark abandon seeking the gods of the ghostland. There was no specific central deity to whom these rites were directed, but early man needed some kind of representation on which to direct his attention and finally the figure of Luçifer emerged. It was the Christian Church which detailed all the horrors of devil worship as later times came to understand it, but one cannot doubt that some witches at this time did seek

The four great witch festivals underlined the offering of thanks for life and fertility with various forms of sexual expression.

concourse with the dark gods and looked to them for more personal reward and power than either the Great Mother or the Horned God offered.

Of their gatherings we know very little except that in obvious fear and trembling—but driven on by man's inexhaustible curiosity—they attempted to contact the dead and raise the black spirits of the night. What we do know for sure, however, is that it was those wayward rites which developed into the notorious Sabbat. We shall return to study it at a later stage in the book.

The occult in early civilizations

As the possessors of dark secrets and a knowledge of the world which was denied to the common man, it is perhaps not surprising to note in succeeding centuries how the stature of the witch-priests and magicians grows for a time in many of the new civilizations.

We have only to look at accounts of the great cities of antiquity such as Carthage and Rome to find witch-priests holding positions of power and authority. In Rome, particularly, the divination of the future—a special attribute of

all early witchcraft practitioners—was considered of great importance to the State, and the men and women carrying out these rituals were consulted by all classes of people from the Emperor downward. (Slaves were, of course, excluded, but wise men often emerged among their ranks.)

Contemporary records tell us that these magicians used a variety of strange items for their divining, including the entrails of beasts, the webs of spiders and live birds. As in past generations, these practitioners guarded their secrets carefully and passed them on only to those who were initiated into their craft.

Some magicians frequently used deception to preserve their sway over the people, and accounts of gatherings of gods appearing and disappearing, spirits that spoke and folk disappearing into thin air can often be put down to projection lamps, concealed assistants and trick chambers.

Records also show us that at this period the traditional idea that the witch must invariably be old and worldly-wise had to be abandoned. Young society women well versed in the occult arts became a feature of the witchcraft scene. Virgil tells us of the beautiful Libyan sorceress who could bewitch 'with both her charms and her magic,' and Ovid rhapsodizes over the occult powers of Colchian Medea. The obvious sexual attraction of these women gave them greater status among men than either the male practitioners or their aging crone counterparts, and several Roman chroniclers have left us with graphic descriptions of rites and orgies conducted by such ladies under the aegis of witchcraft.

Roman witchcraft

Despite the Romans' rational approach to so much of life, they were completely captivated by witchcraft. From the emperor to the lowliest citizen, almost all dabbled in charms, love spells, divination, poisons and curses.

We learn of Augustus, who retained an occultist to interpret his dreams (of which he always took careful note), and the infamous Nero, who strongly encouraged belief in the

In Roman times the idea that the witch was invariably an old crone was disproved in a flurry of beautiful young practitioners.

Several Roman emperors sought knowledge of the future through the interpretation of dreams and the raising of the dead.

supernatural and kept astrologers for himself and his wife, Poppaea.

Just before the advent of Christianity, we see some sinister innovations creeping into Roman witchcraft. The Emperor Commodus, for instance, divined the future by using the entrails of noblemen's sons, a practice he passed on to his successor, Caracalla.

And even when the Empire was converted to the new religion, the rulers still practiced their dark arts, seeking knowledge of the future and assurance of prosperity.

Probably the most notorious of these emperors was Constantine V, who devoted much time, effort and human life to the study of necromancy, 'the raising of the dead.' A good many Romans went in fear of their lives when it was known that the Emperor planned yet another of his regular rituals, for he believed human sacrifice was an integral part of the

ceremony and was not particular about whose corpse should find its way on to his altar—as long as the person had not been dead for more than a few hours and could be relied upon to contain a sound heart and sturdy entrails!

Constantine's rituals frequently turned into orgies of drinking and debauchery, and in some later histories it is his licentiousness for which he is condemned rather than his gruesome occultism!

It is interesting to note that it was at this time that the authorities themselves began to make a clear distinction between 'white' and 'black' magic. While the former was permitted, indeed encouraged, the latter was condemned—although, needless to say, it was practiced as widely as ever by all in a position to get away with it! 'Black' magic in fact provided an added diversion in the search for debauchery and perversion which was so much a part of Imperial life. As one scholar has noted: 'Probably at no other period of history in the West was the practice of magic more rife than in the early centuries of the Christian era.'

Simon Magus

At the time of the outbreak of the Roman persecution of the Christians we find the first references to one of the most important, if ill-defined, figures in the whole history of witchcraft, Simon Magus. Magus, who claimed to be 'the great power of God' and undoubtedly possessed considerable occult power, was much interested in the new religion of the Christ and was indeed baptized into the faith—probably hoping to learn the secrets of the miracles which were attracting so much attention.

During the rule of Claudius, Magus moved to Rome, in company with his mistress, Helena, who he said was a 'heavenly intelligence' he had set free. He continued to practice his arts and was soon regarded with fear and admiration. His powers were such that by the time the new emperor, Nero, was installed he could count not only the ruler but most people in the State as his followers. Magus's main stumbling block to complete domination, however, was the Apostle Peter, who constantly challenged his power

The defeat of the master magician and occultist, Simon Magus, at the hands of the Apostle Peter in Rome

and in fact caused his downfall in what must be one of history's most spectacular public deaths.

Despite Nero's obvious belief in Magus, he demanded that the wizard should perform one special miracle in front of the Roman people—a challenge which he was quick to take up. He said he would prove he was as powerful as God by rising up into the heavens. The Forum was chosen as the site for this display of power. When the populace were assembled—Nero seated in his imperial box—Magus appeared in the arena. With a great sense of the theatrical, he flung wide his arms and—sure enough—began to rise slowly upward. The audience watched dumbfounded. But unknown to the magician, Peter had slipped into the crowds, and as Magus rose up to the highest tiers of the Forum, the Apostle knelt, prayed and made the sign of the cross. Almost immediately the wizard's ascent was checked and he began spiraling down to earth, to crash in a bloody heap at Nero's feet.

Strangely, the influence of Simon Magus did not die with this humiliation. His reputation had spread before him through the Roman Empire and his practices were to form the basis nearly half a century later for a sect of magicians known as the Ophites.

Witches in Britain

With their minds steeped in 'white' and 'black' magic, it is only to be expected that the Romans were quick to see either in the countries they conquered. Their historians make numerous references to magic and occult rituals being observed throughout Europe, but probably nowhere else was the practice as apparent as in Britain.

It is not really surprising that the Old Religion—as witchcraft was now being called—should have continued to survive there among the scattered peasantry. Worship of any kind on a national scale was almost impossible with the constant changing of overlords. The Romans noted the existence of the witch-priests and wise men and reported that they could predict the future and cure illness with their spells and incantations.

The Britons, naturally enough resentful toward their conquerors, were not prepared to share their own carefully evolved rites, so because they lacked reliable historians and scholars of their own, we do not know as much about early witchcraft in Britain as we might wish.

Whatever attitude the Romans took toward these practitioners, the local people regarded them more with reverence than fear. However, they were capable of turning their magic against gullible Roman soldiery, and there are several accounts of witches being flogged or executed for 'working magic against mighty Rome.'

Some authorities have contended that there was an overlap at this period between the Old Religion and the rites of the Druids—and certainly contemporary druidic rites contained a considerable amount of magic.

Strabo, a Greek historian of the first century B.C., wrote that in Ireland there were rites conducted by Druid 'enchanters' which were 'similar to the orgies of Samothrace.' But however closely linked the two practices were—and there is little doubt that both were well supported by the populace—neither group was deterred from following its beliefs by threats from the invaders.

In Britain the witch-priests and Druids held considerable sway and jealously guarded their secrets from the Roman conquerors.

The beginnings of persecution

Even the arrival of Christianity in Britain in the fourth century was to have little immediate effect on the practice of witchcraft. The population was so scattered and illiterate that the Christian missionaries were faced with centuries of work to bring conversion to all—and meanwhile the ever-present wise men and women were ready with magical skills. Indeed for a time Christianity compromised with the Old Religion, and we find many references to temples with altars to both the Christian God and those of witchcraft.

There was little change through the next few centuries and even the priests' threats of hell-fire for unbelievers were to small avail. In fact, the authorities were often hard pressed to define what witchcraft actually was, so with the priests calling the practice a superstitious relic which education would in time remove, witches had little to fear.

But when the Church became a world power its attitude to the Old Religion changed radically. Christianity was now

The heads of bulls and stags were often worn by the witches and gave rise to the stories of devils appearing at their meetings.

the State religion and as such demanded to be the only one. So witchcraft's relegation to the status of an underground cult was inevitable, but as it did not share the Church's desire for mass converts it was quite prepared to function quietly without temples and public ceremony.

However, with the coming of the Middle Ages, the Church mounted a crusade throughout Europe against heresy in all its forms—and while before it had chosen to overlook witchcraft, it now began the persecution which was to last in one form or another for several centuries.

In various ecclesiastical reports of the period we find reference to the witchcraft practices outlawed by the Church. The clergy frowned particularly on dressing in the skin and head of a stag (or bull) 'because this is devilish' and on putting children on the housetop (or in the oven!) 'to ensure them health.' (Some authorities consider the former custom explains the many accounts in witch history of the Devil himself appearing at gatherings.) Other practices—divination, sacrifice, the making of philters, the raising of storms and the attempted evocation of evil spirits—were all deemed heretical and punishable by fines or flogging.

The Witch of Berkeley

Many stories about specific witches were current in Europe at this period. Almost impossible to confirm or deny, they have come down to us in tale or song, like this account from England of the Witch of Berkeley. It is particularly interesting because it is one of the earliest in which the Devil makes a pact and actually appears in 'human' form.

According to the legend, on her deathbed the Witch of Berkeley confessed that her considerable wealth had come to her through 'selling' her soul to the Devil some years before. She implored her friends to perform certain rituals to prevent demons carrying off her body. First they must sew her corpse in the hide of a stag and place it in a stone sarcophagus, sealing this with molten lead and binding it with chains. Fifty priests were then to be summoned to conduct mass for her soul, while another 50 were to sing dirges for the protection of her body. All this was to continue for three days and nights, after which she would have avoided the conditions of her pact.

All the instructions were painstakingly observed but, according to the *Flories Historiarum,* a host of demons broke into the church on both the first and second nights and attempted to open the coffin, being beaten off by the combined effects of the lead sealing of the sarcophagus and the priestly worship.

On the third night, however, a 'hideous specter, a devil in gigantic form and of baleful countenance' appeared during the last rites and, ignoring the frantic singing, bellowed out that the woman was to come with him. A female voice was then heard to reply that she could not move as she was held fast in the sealed coffin. With one blow the Devil swept aside the priests, severed the chains and pushed open the sepulcher. The priests watched helplessly as the figure then drew the old woman from the coffin, strode with her to the shattered door and disappeared into the night. By all accounts the corpse of the unfortunate Witch of Berkeley was never recovered.

The famous legend of the Witch of Berkeley, who was seized from her coffin by her master, the Devil, and some of his demons

Witch mania in Europe

Throughout Europe, then, the battle was being joined against the witches, for no other crime than not being avowedly Christian in their beliefs. In France, Germany and Italy we read of witches being severely punished and commanded to 'turn to God away from heresy.' Once engendered, there was no way to stop the flames of witch mania—kindled as they were on fanaticism, fear and superstition—and the severity of punishment increased at an alarming rate until torture and death were commonplace.

The Inquisition, which began in 1233, crystallized this movement. It was established by the Catholic Church to search out and punish 'false doctrine and heresy,' including witchcraft. The system openly encouraged informers, and the accused were first brought before the secular courts and when found guilty—as they always were—taken to the local inquisitors, usually Dominican friars. To be charged with practicing witchcraft and brought before these 'men of God' meant torture and almost invariably death; records from

Illustrations from a tract on tortures of the Inquisition (1651)

the ensuing centuries clearly show the severity with which the Inquisition acted.

In France, for instance, during the reign of Henry III, in the late sixteenth century, over 30,000 executions took place, and in Germany, in just the small bishopric of Würzburg, 157 men, women and children were burned to death in 1627. (Germany, in fact, was to suffer more than any other country during the witchcraft persecutions; Scotland took second place and France third.) In Hungary in 1628, 15 people were simultaneously burned alive on three fires, and in Spain fear split families apart and many victims went to the stake on the evidence of a relation or close friend.

Throughout each of these countries the inquisitor's net spread wide, carrying to the stake peasants, noblemen, the sick, the young and even, on occasions, the clergy. Wherever one went the tales of horror mounted, and no one could be sure of his life from day to day. A careless word, a strange action, and death could be just a whispered word away.

Once begun, the system was to continue for 200 years—and leave a blot on the story of humanity which can never be erased.

The inquistors' 'textbook'

The inquisitors' 'textbook' was the *Malleus Maleficarum* (The Hammer of the Witches). Undoubtedly the most important work ever written on witchcraft and its 'treatment,' the book clung tenaciously to the principle of Exodus xxii. 18, that 'Thou shalt not suffer a witch to live.' Published in 1486, it was the work of two Dominican priests, Jakob Sprenger and Heinrich Kramer, both considerable scholars but blindly and passionately opposed to witchcraft.

In the *Malleus Maleficarum* they recorded how to seek out suspected witches, how to try them (with notes on the various necessary and brutal forms of torture) and the required punishment. By modern standards the book is hopelessly one-sided, lacking in simple logic and guaranteed to inflame any persecution—but it offered *carte blanche* to the inquisitors and its acceptance was immediate and widespread. It seemed to matter little to them that Kramer had used deception to start a bloody witch hunt in the Tyrol and that Sprenger was disowned by his university for denying all the humanities he had previously preached.

Coinciding with the publication of this book we find the first real difficulties in accurately reporting the history of the Old Religion. The confessions and accounts which exist are in the main most misleading and we can only conjecture about what really happened.

It would seem that the followers of the ancient craft at first readily admitted to their beliefs. Indeed, as they intended no affront to the Church—merely preferring to observe ancient, pre-Christian rituals—one can understand why they believed the Church, preaching 'love and tolerance to all men,' would see their point of view. But it did not—nor did it accept the witches' explanation of the origin of their cult. In the Horned God it saw the personification of the Devil, the person it was most dedicated to attack, and in the fertility rites a deliberate outrage to the teaching of Jesus Christ. To get the witches to accept this interpretation it was prepared to go to any lengths.

Jakob Sprenger and Hëinrich Kramer, authors of *Malleus Maleficarum:* one of the inquisitors' most important aids

SPRENGER
KRAMER

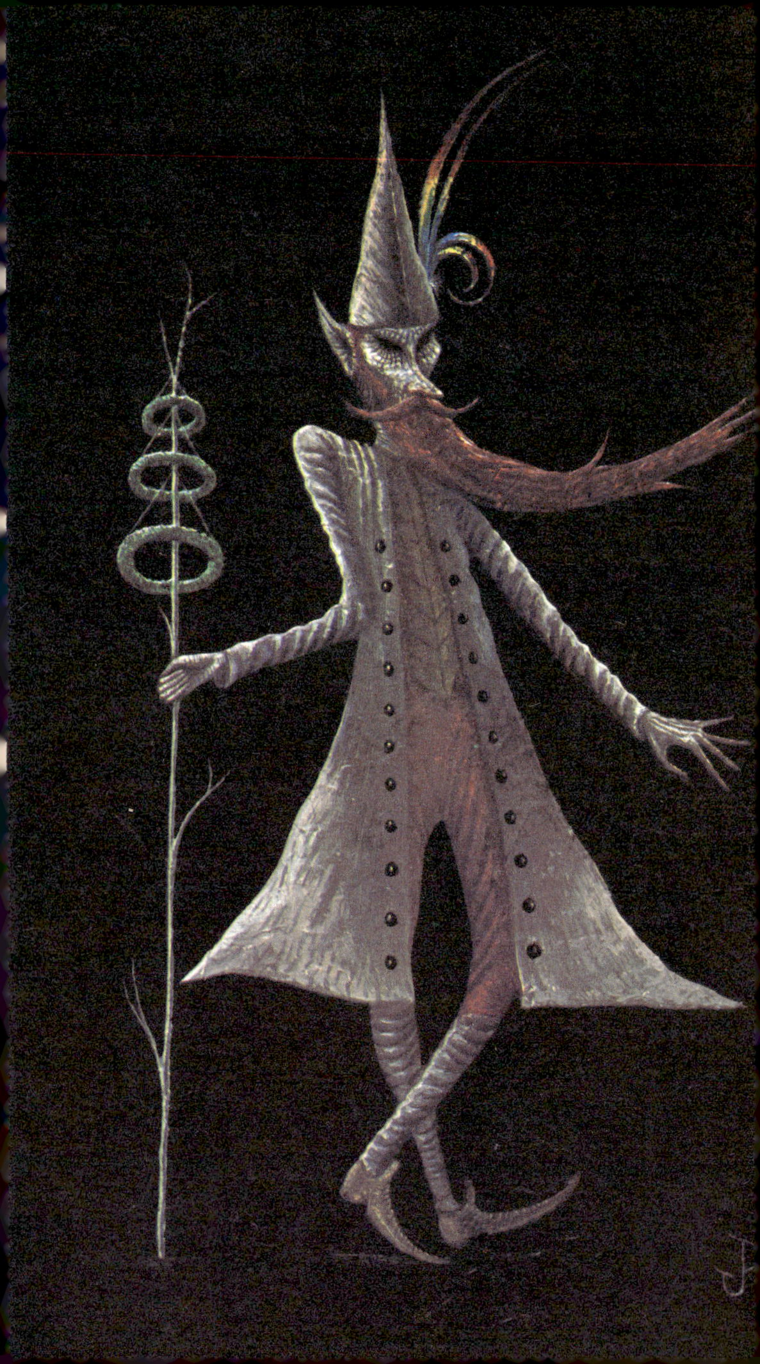

Centers of devil worship

In examining the confessions of European witches tried at this time, we discover that there were supposedly three sites most frequently used by the practitioners for their gatherings, or Sabbats: on the Brocken Mountain in Germany, in a grove near Benevento in Italy, and on a deserted stretch of land in the heart of Jordan.

We know most about the German site. There is a plentiful supply of illustrations—the majority completely fanciful—showing the devil figure sitting on top of the mountain receiving homage from his worshipers. Dancing, feasting, outrage and indiscriminate sexual intercourse with man and demon are depicted as common features of this Sabbat—plus certain other elements of an obscene nature that are suggested in some of the secret illustrations withdrawn from public exhibition in the British and Leipzig Museums. In Italy the revelers were equally abandoned and had a predilection for showing homage to the Devil by acts of bestiality, while farther south in Jordan nudity was the order of the meetings and the excessive eating (primarily of the very sickly 'witch butter') probably accounts for the large number of exceedingly fat men and women present!

Another site that has been widely recorded is 'a large delicate meadow whereof you can see no end' at Mora in Sweden. Here, apart from their revels, the faithful were also busily engaged in building a stone house 'to preserve themselves on the Day of Judgment' but this, according to the reports, 'was always tumbling down once they had finished the walls thereof.' These people were also able to summon the Devil in person by merely shouting: 'Beelzebub, come forth!' And when he did appear, the figure 'wore a red beard and breeches to match, a gray coat and stockings, and a peaked cap with cocks' feathers in it.'

At all these gatherings it was said the Devil baptized new followers—entering their names in blood in a huge black book—and then had them dance around him until they collapsed, at which point he beat them with their broomsticks until they rose or he decided they had had enough!

The Devil as seen by some of his 16th-century Swedish followers

Witchcraft in high places

A great many extraordinary stories exist about the practice of witchcraft in 'high places' in Europe, but probably the most dramatic of all began with a nun who was alleged to have secretly indoctrinated many of her sisters in the Untezell Convent near Würzburg.

The woman, Sister Maria Renata, was said to have been secretly initiated into witchcraft at the age of 13, and in obedience to her guardians entered a convent six years later. By stealth and cunning she not only managed to continue her 'black' magic but also gave the impression that she was an honest and diligent servant of God and so became a subprioress. For 40 years she worked 'all manner of dark magic' against the nuns, causing them to have seizures and cry out against God at night—at which she, being in charge, would beat the unfortunate victims.

Her downfall eventually came when she caused six nuns to be possessed at once; despite all the attentions of the

The Nuns of Würzburg, who were said to have come under the spell of their subprioress, a secret practitioner of the dark arts

other sisters—and a priest especially summoned—the women remained in this state for some days, calling out in strange, tormented voices: 'Our time is come! Our time is come! We cannot lie longer hid.' Cross-examined afterward, all recalled close contact with Sister Maria just before their possession.

The subprioress was seized and under torture said she had been seduced by Satan at the age of 11, learned the secrets of evil magic at 13 and at 19 been ordered to infiltrate a convent. She said she had frequently left the convent at night, danced in the nude at a local Sabbat and copulated with all and sundry. She also admitted that she had attended gatherings near Vienna where 'members of the nobility and high citizenry were present.'

Her confession painted a picture of half a nation practicing witchcraft and the dark arts, and indeed her story parallels many more from other countries during the sixteenth and seventeenth centuries. She was sentenced to death and taken to Marienberg, where she was first beheaded and then her body burned. After her death many people in high places went in fear of exposure in case the Black Sister of Wurzburg had named them in her *extremis*.

The Witchcraft Act of 1563

In England, too, there was good reason to suspect that people in all strata of society were involved in witchcraft. Indeed a group of dissatisfied noblemen trying to work a spell against Queen Elizabeth were discovered making a wax effigy of the monarch by some diligent soldiers.

The Queen herself played an important part in the story of witchcraft: she was responsible for the introduction of the Witchcraft Act of 1563. It prescribed death by hanging for 'employing or exercising witchcraft with the intent to kill or destroy' and a year's imprisonment for 'hurting persons in bodie or to waste and destroy goods' (with a rider that the prisoner could be put in the stocks once a quarter for 'the space of six hours' as an example to all). As a result, thousands of old crones were hauled before courts and condemned on the flimsiest evidence. It is a sad memorial to the first Elizabeth that during the 45 years of her reign, more trials for the practicing of witchcraft were conducted than

James I produced a study of devil worship, *Demonology* (1597), and wrote the brutal 1604 Witchcraft Act into the statute books.

A contemporary illustration of King James interrogating suspected witches at a trial in North Berwick, Scotland, in 1590

throughout the whole of the seventeenth century.

Nor was the hostile climate toward witchcraft helped by James I, her successor. He forced Parliament to repeal Elizabeth's Act in 1604 in favor of a bill which prescribed death for a much wider list of offenses. James had become interested in witchcraft early in his life and in 1597 in his *Demonology* stated categorically: 'the works of Satan are most certainly practiced and the instruments thereof merit most severely to be punished.' The work was widely used after the introduction of the new Act—which itself was applied at several famous trials, including those in Lancashire in 1612 and 1633 and the series of committals in eastern England in 1645. But for all his early enthusiasm, James came to doubt that the trials gave a true picture of witchcraft and to feel that much greater enquiry was necessary. Nonetheless his harsh Act remained on the statutes for over a hundred years.

The witch finders

In the years which followed the introduction of King James's Act, a new profession emerged, a group of men dedicated to discovering witchcraft 'wherever it may be hid.' These men, known as witch finders, often had little more qualification for their work than a blind hatred of what they believed to be the practice of evil, but they engendered a very real fear in others. No simple countryman or woman dared to challenge them in case he or she was maliciously accused of being in league with the Devil.

The most famous of these men was Matthew Hopkins, an unsuccessful English lawyer, who in 1645 and 1646 'sent to the gallows more witches than all the other witch hunters in England.' He ranged throughout the eastern counties of England, using as his campaign slogan the passage in King James's *Demonology* which stated that all witches had familiars. In each case he brought to trial, he claimed to have actually seen these familiars or imps and described them as resembling dogs, cats or small mice and varying in size from 'no bigger than a fly to that of a full-grown hound.'

Hopkins's most famous trial was that at Chelmsford, Essex (see page 102), where he used his favorite methods of torture, 'swimming' and 'pricking.' But in 1646 his bloody career was brought to an abrupt end by a Huntingdonshire priest, John Gaule—one of the first to try to understand witchcraft and the delusions which surrounded it. Gaule publicly exposed the indiscriminate hunts, and even Hopkins's reply, a pamphlet entitled *Discovery of Witches*, could not help him.

People were suddenly sickened by the wholesale murder that was being sanctioned in their name, and credence of all Hopkins's claims ceased. Deprived of his authority, the witch finder had to retire and within a year had died under mysterious circumstances. The most widely held view is that he was a victim of tuberculosis; other accounts have it that his neighbors, tired of listening to his boasting, seized him one morning and subjected him to the punishment he had given so many others—a 'swimming' in the local pond—from which he died. The truth will never be known.

The infamous English witch finder, Matthew Hopkins

Matthew
Hopkins

Some of the terrible instruments of torture shown in a 16th-century pamphlet compiled about the German witch trials

The torture of witches

To be in league with the Devil and thus sin against God was widely held to be the most heinous of crimes. Extreme measures were needed to combat it, and Jean Bodin noted in *De la démonomanie des sorciers* (1580): 'to punish the most detestable crimes of which the human mind can conceive one must punish with the utmost rigor the witches.'

The inquisitors believed that no witch should be executed without first making her confess, and that this admission of guilt should be made under torture 'so that it can be presumed to come from the heart.' In most of Europe the style of examination was first to threaten the victim with torture if she or he did not confess, next show the implements and then strip the body naked. If this produced no result, the unfortunate was turned over to the torturer.

The rack was undeniably the most effective and widely

used of all implements, although thumbscrews were often used on women. In Europe, strappado was a common torture. The victim's arms were tied behind him with a rope attached to a pulley and he was then hoisted in the air—weights sometimes being attached to his feet to intensify the pain. Squassation was an even more brutal version; the prisoner was dropped from a height and jerked to a stop just short of the floor. This was an extreme measure: one application usually dislocated the limbs and three almost invariably killed.

An examination of old prints and records clearly shows the variety and ingenuity of the many tortures employed. As the German Jesuit, Friedrich von Spee, wrote in the sixteenth century: 'The result is the same whether the witch confesses or not. If she confesses, her guilt is clear: she is executed. If she does not confess, the torture is repeated—twice, thrice, four times. In exceptional crimes the torture is not limited in duration, severity or frequency . . . indeed she can never clear herself.'

The horrifying water ordeal, from an illustration of 1651

A change of climate

At last, through all this terrible bigotry and persecution, came a ray of common sense—in the person of a British king, Charles II. Always skeptical about much of what was said of witchcraft and disapproving of the indiscriminate butchery employed against those suspected of practicing it, he made his feelings well known on his accession to the throne in 1660. The effect was not long in being felt.

However, so deeply embedded in the English tradition were the trials that even the King could not hope to stop them in a matter of a few years. But his objective approach led to rational principles being applied to the subject instead of hatred and prejudice.

Through Charles's reign and those which immediately followed, the climate gradually changed, and in the year 1717 we find the last recorded committal for witchcraft in England. This case, brought by 25 people against an old woman and her son, was tried before the Leicester Assizes.

Ducking was a popular method of witch trial in many countries.

The witch prickers—the middle knife has a retractable blade

The pair were accused of causing illness by casting spells, possessing familiars and being able to change their shapes at will.

The first part of the trial took the traditional form of a 'ducking,' and as they did not drown they were felt to be in league with the Devil. The old woman was also 'pricked,' the practice so popular with the witch finders.

The instrument used was a long, pointed blade which was applied to any part of the body suspected of concealing the devil's mark (the sign allegedly placed on the witch at her initiation) and if any such area did not bleed or was painless this was considered proof of complicity. (To further their trade, many of the witch finders devised instruments with hollow shafts and retractable blades, so as to ensure conviction.) In the Leicester case the old woman had several immune areas and these—with the discovery of two pieces of flesh 'like the paps of a cat'—were enough to earn her conviction. The grand jury, however, was not satisfied and later overruled the decision because of the lack of any real evidence. Justice, it seemed, had at last lost its blindfold.

Repeal of the witchcraft acts

The lead that Charles II had given was soon taken up throughout the British Isles and Europe, and by the time George III became King of Great Britain witchcraft was being dismissed in many quarters as 'superstitious nonsense.'

In 1736 the Witchcraft Act which James I had introduced was repealed, and in its place came a law which decreed imprisonment for one year and 'to be stood in the stocks each quarter' for anyone practicing 'any kind of witchcraft, sorcery, enchantment or conjuration.' This effectively ended the treatment of witchcraft as a capital crime and remained unchanged on the English statute books until 1951.

In Scotland the law against the witches was also being changed, but there was considerable resistance; not for nothing had the country gained the reputation of being second only to Germany in the severity of its witchcraft persecution. North of the Border, stories of strange practices proliferated. Few had not heard the legends of a coven at Forres which regularly roasted a wax effigy of King Duffus over a fire, apparently 'causing him to be sore afflicted in his body,' or of the notorious devil-worshiper William,

One Scottish devil worshiper, Lord Soulis, was boiled in oil.

Lord Soulis, who conducted dire orgies at his castle in Roxburgh and so revolted his neighbors that they seized him, rolled him up in sheets of lead and boiled him to death!

There was also a long list of brutal witch trials in Scotland at which innocent and guilty alike had been committed to the stake—after subjection to the most bestial torture. Another account worthy of mention concerns the great churchman John Knox, who was said to have attempted necromancy; the experiment went horribly wrong and caused the Devil himself to rise—the sight of whom is said to have made one of Knox's companions die of fright!

Throughout the rest of Europe, too, the pattern was the same. In Germany a reign of persecution which had brought at least 100,000 suspected witches to trial and death began to decline, but it was not to be finally halted until 1775 with the case of Anna Maria Schwägel, to which we shall return later. In France, Italy, Spain and throughout Scandinavia (where the level of hysteria was much the same), education and rationality gradually overruled bigotry and brought repeal to the majority of the witchcraft statutes.

The reign of terror was over—and, as we shall see, the practice of witchcraft in its ancient form as a fertility religion was to rise again.

THE FACETS OF WITCHCRAFT

The witch in art

Artists have traditionally had an interest in witchcraft, which is hardly surprising if you consider for a moment how superstition and fear of the unknown still enthrall us even today. The witch in art is certainly an absorbing topic. Our galleries, libraries and museums are full of pictures which, if not always accurate enough to satisfy the objective researcher, can tell much of social climates and conditions.

Despite the variety of the evidence, it is nonetheless surprising to see that the witch—the female, that is—has remained much the same in portraits through the years. The traditional idea of the witch as an old hag (the word deriving from the Anglo-Saxon *haegtesse*, a female demon), a filthy old woman clothed in rags, can be traced right back to the earliest recorded history. Very much in this genre are drawings such as that of the notorious Mother Damnable, a seventeenth-century witch who lived in appalling squalor in Kentish Town, London—but was apparently gifted with the art of curing sickness, making prophecies and even raising the dead! David Teniers the Younger, a Flemish artist working in the seventeenth century, painted several masterpieces in the same tradition, depicting witches as being withered, extremely ugly and invariably in the company of the most hideous demons and familiars.

The erotic element is very evident in many witchcraft paintings, particularly those which show the sabbat orgies and neophytes being admitted to the cult—stripped naked and under the probing hands of men, women and devils. These pictures of the Sabbat have contributed considerably to many of the most enduring misconceptions about witchcraft. For though a few of the artists had a practical knowledge of the cult, the vast majority were letting their imaginations loose on the highly colored legends and stories of their time. Small wonder, then, the pictures show witches flying, sacrificing—sometimes eating—children, and conjuring up demons with whom they copulate.

Mother Damnable, the 17th-century London witch of ill-repute

Mallie Babbe, the handsome sorceress of Haarlem by Frans Hals

All the fantasies that surrounded the Sabbat were probably best summarized in Brueghel's painting of this gathering. It is alive with demons, imps, magic circles made of human flesh (plus a cauldron in which to boil it!), sky-riding humans and animals and even the Devil himself, who is about to rise up through the ground from the flaming depths of hell.

For the other side of the story there is the magnificent frontispiece to John Webster's *The Displaying of Supposed Witchcraft* (1677), which shows a figure in bed dreaming all Brueghel's fantasies and captioned: 'It is clear that one addlepate dreams up in his own mind all the supposed deeds of a thousand witches.'

The great Spanish painter Goya was also much intrigued by witchcraft. The *Caprichos* engravings and the 'Black' paintings reflect his interest, and the former surely rank as the most sardonic comment on witchcraft ever made.

The witch trials and tortures are also graphically recorded

in art, and most of these paintings from the fifteenth to the eighteenth century spare us few details of the brutality exercised by the authorities on their luckless prisoners. An unknown master depicted the whole range of torture employed by the Germans in a book published in 1631, in one example showing a male witch having his legs broken and neck lacerated by an iron collar. Yet another painting—done in 1587 by a Frenchman—shows a man being pressed to death under a heap of stones while around him female members of his coven are stripped naked and shaved of bodily hair to receive the attention of the rack and some hideous-looking 'iron shoes' that crush the feet.

In the Bodleian Library at Oxford there are a number of nineteenth-century prints showing practitioners of 'white' magic being consulted by peasants for advice about their crops and herds—one also has a love problem—but again all these witches are old, ugly and live in terrible squalor.

However, variety abounds in the history of witchcraft and we have only to turn for a moment to other sources to find some handsome—indeed beautiful—witches.

Witchcraft is an important theme in Goya's 'Black' period (1819–23).

Mother Shipton, who was allegedly the offspring of a union between the Devil and a witch, is shown in several paintings as a striking, open-featured woman, demurely attired and hardly looking likely to be involved in the most diabolical traffic with the Fiend, as stories would have us believe.

Several other artists were also at pains to show there were beautiful witches in existence; Hans Baldung Grien, the Austrian, made a series of pictures filled with young, voluptuous practitioners, and one of the most widely reproduced of all witch canvases is Albrecht Dürer's picture of four beautiful, young naked sorceresses. Frans Hals has shown us that even the older witches need not necessarily be ugly and his picture of Mallie Babbe, the sorceress of Haarlem, depicts a charming, comely woman anyone might be pleased to have as a relative.

From the same period in Germany comes an oil painting, now in the Leipzig Museum, of a flaxen-haired girl being taken to the stake amid jeering crowds and described as the fairest maid in all Wurzburg.' And in the British Museum there is a delicate line-drawing of the late sixteenth century that shows a young witch anointing herself with 'flying ointment' and causing a small demon crouching in one corner to stare open-mouthed at her beauty.

Of course the most popular, least accurate representation has been the old lady with a black, pointed hat and flowing cloak who possesses a broomstick on which she flies and a cat who can change shape. From this notion—now confined to children's fairy tales and folklore studies—came the simile 'as ugly as a witch' and the directive given by many an opponent of witchcraft that ugliness was to be taken as an important proof when examining a suspected witch.

There is, needless to say, some truth in all the paintings mentioned. Witches came from all strata of society and there is no good reason why one section should have been more blessed with beauty than another. As one critic has said: 'Why should Satan have always had to make do with second best where beauty is concerned?'

The witch through modern eyes: 'changeability' is an ancient belief.

Familiars

Inextricably linked with the history of witchcraft are the mysterious witch familiars. Often depicted in old prints as resembling small cats or mice, these tiny creatures were said to take many forms and be the instruments used by the witches to carry out their evil tasks.

It is interesting to note that they were only recorded in any number in England and Scotland; very few accounts of their appearance are to be found in thc United States, continental Europe or other areas.

The creatures were supposedly given to the witch after she had made a pact with the Devil. In a confession taken from the St. Osyth witch trials in 1582 we find this description of four 'spirits': 'One he, like a gray cat, is called Tittey; the second, like a black cat, is called Jack; one she, like a black toad, is called Pigin; and the other, like a black lamb, is called Tyffin . . . the two he spirits were to punish and kill

A witch, and with her some of the creatures which have been named as imps or familiars—all quite ordinary, everyday animals

unto death, and the two shes were to punish with lameness and other diseases of bodily harm.'

The claim to have seen familiars—or imps as they are sometimes called—was for a long time a crucial factor in English witch trials, and we have plentiful evidence of prosecutors producing dead cats, dogs, mice and even flies that had in life supposedly been gifted with devilish powers used in the service of the accused.

The witch finder Matthew Hopkins repeatedly swore to having actually seen familiars in the homes of the people he brought to trial, and he even avowed on one occasion to having seen a woman suckling a mole-shaped imp.

A famous print of the witch finder shows him with two accused witches who are pointing out their familiars and naming them. The picture, like most other contemporary illustrations, lends weight to the belief that the familiars were nothing more than domestic pets gratefully seized upon by the crusading authorities as a convenient extra piece of evidence to lead yet another unfortunate woman or man to the gibbet.

The coven

Scholars have argued at great length for many years about whether the witches gathered in groups, or covens, to pay homage to the gods. I subscribe to the case which Dr. Margaret Murray presents in *The Witch Cult in Western Europe.* She believes that the coven developed from the groups of Stone-Age dwellers who first began the worship of the fertility and hunting gods, and that the witches continued to meet occasionally during the years of persecution.

Dr. Murray also thinks the traditional number of members in a coven was 13 and supports her case with examples from France, Germany, Scotland and England. She says the word was first used in 1662 when the Scottish witch Isobel Gowdie told her examiners that 'there are 13 persons in each coven.' However, it seems probable that the number varied greatly over the years. Other scholars—notably Montague Summers in his book *History of Witchcraft and*

Through the years of persecution and trial, the true devotees of the Old Religion continued to meet in secret in small covens.

Demonology—state that not only did each coven have a leader or high priest (priestess), but that in certain European countries groups of covens had an overlord or 'chief officer of the witches in the district.'

Opponents have been at pains to point out that most of these authorities used witch confessions as the basis for their theories—and as these were invariably extracted under torture, little reliance can be placed on what was said. But while, probably rightly, they scoff at any suggestion of witchcraft being a worldwide organization, they do overlook the fact that many of those tried for witchcraft knew little if anything about its actual practice and were urged to confess to whatever suited the inquisitors. I am more inclined to the view that the genuine believers in the Old Religion did continue to meet together secretly on a regional basis to counsel about the persecution—and that some of these meetings were known to the ordinary people.

The Sabbat

According to most reliable accounts there were two kinds of meeting attended by the witches: the Esbat, which was an assembly of a small group or coven for 'business' reasons (the discussion of persecution or the laying of spells), and the Sabbat, which was a ritual gathering of a great many witches and their covens to celebrate 'all the joys of their secret beliefs.'

No other topic relating to witchcraft can have been more debated and argued over than the Sabbat.

Obviously it is never going to be possible to categorize those meetings which were inherently good in intent and those which were evil, for our reporters are either terrified and superstitious peasants or else witches tortured to the point of admitting to whatever fantasies the inquisitors might suggest. However, we can be sure—on the authority of scholars such as Dr. Margaret Murray and Montague Summers—that many of them were held by followers of the Old Religion keeping their rituals alive. The rest, it seems reasonable to suppose, were held by evil occultists and magicians for their personal satisfaction and profit. Drugs and potions, of course, were an integral part of both 'white' and 'black' magic, and it is quite possible that many of the Sabbats originated in the drug-stupefied minds of practitioners who never actually left their beds!

It is quite impossible to pinpoint a time when the Sabbat as popularly portrayed first began to be held, and indeed Professor Kurt Seligman is probably closest to the truth when he says: 'The Sabbat became sinister when the old pagan rites were no longer considered the revival of a decayed past but an evil activity born of heresy.'

We know the participants chose their sites with great care (see pages 32–33) and often prepared a place where there were the remains of megalithic monuments. Legend has it that the witches flew by broomstick to these places, but as Dr. Murray says: 'The number of cases vouched for by the persons who actually performed or saw the feat of riding on a stick through the air are disappointingly few.'

There are a number of excellent accounts of Sabbats to be found in books published between the fifteenth and seventeenth centuries. This one, taken from *A Pleasant Treatise of Witches* published in 1673, is typical:

'They (witches) are likewise reported to have each of them a spirit or imp attending on and assigned to them, which never leave those to whom they are subject, but assist and render them all the service they command. These give the witches notice to be ready at all Solemn appointments, and meetings, and then they strive to separate themselves from the company of all other Creatures, not to be seen by any; and night being come, they strip themselves naked, and annoint themselves with their Oyntments. Then are they carryed out of the house, either by the Window, Door or Chimney, mounted on their broomstick or their imps in form of Goat, Sheep or a Dragon, till they arrive at their meeting place, wither all the other Witches and Wizards, each one upon his imps, are also brought.

'Thus brought to the designed place, which is sometimes many hundred miles from their dwellings, they find a great number of others arrived there by the same means; who, before Lucifer takes his place in his Throne as King, do

The half-real, half-illusory world of the medieval Sabbat

Devil worshipers trampled the Cross at the initiation ceremony.

make their accustomed homage, Adoring and Proclaiming him their Lord, and rendering him all Honour.

'This solemnity being finished, they sit at table where no delicate meats are wanting to gratifie their Appetites, all dainties being thither brought in the twinkling of an eye, by those spirits that attend the Assembly. This done at the sound of many pleasant Instruments (for we must expect no Grace in the company of Devils), the table is taken away, and the pleasant consort invites them to a Ball; but the dance is strange, and wonderful, as well as diabolical, for twining themselves back to back, they take one another by the arms and raise each other from the ground, then shake their heads to and fro like Anticks, and turn themselves as if they were mad. Then at last, after this Banquet, Musick and Ball, the lights are put out, and their sleeping Venus awakes, and all do enjoin together for lewd pleasures.

'At last, before Aurora brings back the day, each one

mounts on his broom or spirit and so returns to his respective dwelling place, with that lightness and quickness that in little space they find themselves to be carryed many hundred miles.'

Most reports of the Sabbat drawn from the period follow much the same pattern as this, mingling fact and fantasy, but from them we can draw a number of reasonable conclusions about what actually happened.

For instance, many reports have it that the Devil would arrive in person at the beginning of the proceedings, his body glowing red and surrounded by clouds of sulphur. Pope Gregory IX says otherwise: 'The devil appears to them in the figure of a pale, black-eyed youth with a melancholy aspect and a heart filled with eternal hatred against the Holy Church.' This latter seems much more likely and gives rise to the theory that the devil figure was a man dressed in animal skins who presided over the assembly. Professor Seligman substantiates this and adds: 'Often the disguise was mistaken for the original and before long the fur-clad master of the Sabbat was believed to be Satan in person.'

The feast was a high point of the traditional Sabbat.

There is little doubt that feasts took place at all the gatherings, but one should be skeptical about stories that blood was drunk and the bodies of young children eaten. More likely strong wine or mead was drunk and raw meat eaten to heighten the senses for the sex play to follow. Reports also suggest that many of the feasts were vast and opulent 'when some wealthy person had financed it.'

The initiation of new recruits—be they children brought by their parents, or adults—has come in for considerable comment. At the evil gatherings, it is said, the neophyte had to trample on a crucifix and then (according to St. Hippolytus) repeat: 'I deny the creator of heaven and earth. I deny my baptism. I deny the worship I formerly paid to God. I cleave to thee, Satan, and in thee I believe.' Next came the 'black baptism,' when the candidate was marked, washed in filthy water and given a secret name for use at the Sabbats. Like his fellow practitioners, the new recruit also had to make the special act of obedience, the *osculum obscoenum*

In the dance of adoration the witches moved counterclockwise.

The *osculum obscoenum,* or kiss of shame, was an act of obedience.

—the kiss given to the devil figure's exposed buttocks.

Frenzied dancing brought the proceedings to a climax and 'all threw off their clothes, linked arms and swung round together in huge circles, moving ever to the left,' according to the *Compendium Maleficarum,* published in 1626. Finally the inflamed passions of the naked dancers turned to lust and as the demonologist Pierre de Lancre records: 'the witches gave themselves over to copulation: the son did not spare the mother, neither the brother the sister, nor the father the daughter; incest went on everywhere.'

Some witches confessed that they had been intimate with the Devil himself, but most feared this as 'his member was scaly and caused extreme pain; furthermore his semen was extremely cold.' Certain authorities have since argued with justification that these statements probably arose because women frequently outnumbered men very considerably at

An old woman using a secret formula to summon a demon

the Sabbats and substitute phalli were much employed.

Records of the Sabbats indicate that they were most frequently held on Sunday nights—although any night of the week was permissible. Four Grand Sabbats were held each year (on February 2, June 23, August 1 and December 2) and the usual time to commence was two hours before midnight so that the activities were at their peak as the new day started. According to other sources, dawn, or 'the crowing of a cock,' was the signal for the revelers to depart.

At the evil Sabbats it is said the faithful were given certain secret formulas for summoning up demons—of which there were many thousands. Demonologists have credited these creatures with a variety of powers: Asmodeus 'the prince of wantons,' for instance, could be sent to lure man 'with his swine of luxuriousness,' whereas Astaroth 'tempts men with idleness and sloth.' One noted scholar, Johan Weyer (1515–88) even claimed to have counted 'all the devils in Hell's legions' and announced the grand total as '7,405,926 demons and 72 princes of hell.'

Because of the preoccupation with sex at the Sabbat, capacity for intercourse was of great concern to all. Innumerable aphrodisiac potions were available, the ingredients of some of these being truly extraordinary: bats' blood, cats' brains, spiders, frogs, and various herbs—all mixed together and chanted over with due ceremony.

At the Sabbats conducted by the followers of the Old Religion, certain medicines were prepared that had remarkable curative properties, and some of these have since formed the basis of prescriptions which have been developed by modern scientists and chemists. But at evil Sabbats, devotees would often be called upon to take part in some mass ritual to harm a chosen victim.

These, then, are the elements of the Sabbat. It will probably never reveal all its secrets but its origin in the fertility rites of primitive man is not difficult to trace, nor is it hard to see why later worshipers sometimes perverted it.

Two famous demons as portrayed by Collin de Plancy (1863)

[illegible]

[illegible]

The pact with the Devil

The first instance we have of a pact with the Devil, so often regarded as the very root of all witchcraft, is far back in antiquity. At first the making of a bond whereby the soul is given up to the Evil One after a specified time in return for wealth and honor was merely an oral arrangement, but our Devil must have tired of this (or had too many people trying to break their agreement) for after the twelfth century it is invariably written—and in blood.

Not surprisingly there are very few of these pacts extant and the validity of the whole subject must be questioned. However, we should examine one pact which some scholars believe to have been genuinely executed, if not finalized. It concerns the infamous priest of Loudun, Urbain Grandier, who was accused in 1633 of having bewitched the local nuns and dabbled in the black arts (see pages 106–107). A copy of the pact, which was found among Grandier's papers after his arrest and is now lodged in the Bibliothèque Nationale in Paris, is shown on the opposite page and translated reads:

'My Lord and Master, I own you for my God; I promise to serve you while I live, and from this hour I renounce all other gods and Jesus Christ and Mary and all the Saints of Heaven and the Catholic, Apostolic and Roman Church, and all the goodwill thereof and the prayers which might be made for me. I promise to adore you and do you homage at least three times a day and to do the most evil that I can and to lead into evil as many persons as shall be possible to me, and heartily I renounce the Christ, Baptism, and all the merits of Jesus Christ; and, in case I should desire to change, I give you my body and soul, and my life as holding it from you, having dedicated it for ever without any will to repent. Signed URBAIN GRANDIER in his blood.'

Of course if we accept the possibility of a pact with the Devil, it is not unreasonable that he should come for his own in due time (between seven and nine years) and indeed there are stories of futile attempts to avoid the ultimate encounter by those who had bloodied the 'devil parchment.'

Grandier's pact. It is written in Latin, from right to left, and signed in blood. The cosignators were alleged to be devils.

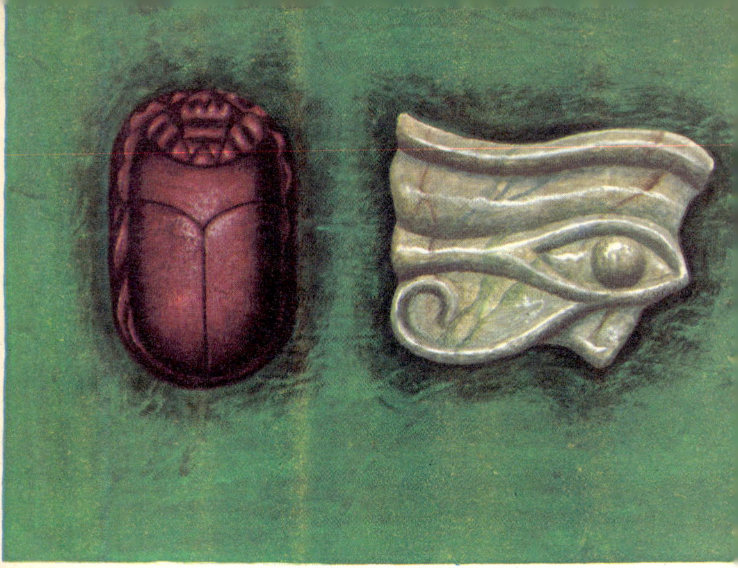

Pre-Christian charms: the scarab (*left*) and the Eye of Horus (*right*)

Witch charms

Some dabblers in the dark arts were said to believe that it was possible to avoid being carried off by the Devil after making a pact with him by confronting him with a charm such as a crucifix or Holy Bible. True or not, a whole range of charms have become associated with witchcraft.

According to Leonardo Vairo in his *Trois livres des charmes, sorcelages ou enchantements* (1583), charms were 'invented by devils to satisfy their rage against mankind,' and the notorious *Malleus Maleficarum* listed seven rules to determine good and evil charms.

These could take many forms, from the traditional chanted formula to wax figures which were used to inflict pain or death on the victim, amulets worn on the wrist and little medallions hung around the neck. This last type was much frowned on in many countries, and in Scotland, for instance, we find that the wearing of a token not immediately identifiable with Christianity was punishable by death until the repeal of the witchcraft laws. The witches showed amazing

Later and most effective antiwitch charms. The bottle contains herbs.

ingenuity when selecting material for their charms, and the items they drew on ranged from metals and herbs to blood, twine, pubic hair and even hogs' dung!

We know from several trials that the witches possessed a variety of charm ointments which they concealed on their bodies and then applied before torture began. There can be little doubt that these had a strong drug content to reduce pain. (Another ointment in this category was the type allegedly used by the witches to fly.)

Mankind also sought to protect itself against the dark powers by devising antiwitch charms. Thomas Aquinas wrote: 'To attach holy words about the neck, provided they contain nothing false or suspect, is certainly not unlawful.' Among the earliest protective symbols—predating Christianity—were the scarab and the Eye of Horus; both were credited with the power 'to drive away demons and spirits.' Later charms sometimes made use of items as unlikely as those of the witches, but by far the most effective were said to be 'herbs, the silver crucifix and the good words of the Bible.'

The evil eye

In return for their dedication, one of the powers which was apparently entrusted to witches was the ability to cause suffering or death by use of the evil eye. This power, sometimes called 'overlooking,' enabled the witch to inflict punishment by a mere glance and is mentioned even in the earliest histories. The use of this remarkable attribute was said to have been revealed by the Devil himself with the following instructions: 'If you bear ill-will to anybody, look on them with open eyes and pray evil for them in my name and you will get your heart's desires.'

The Romans took the evil eye very seriously and at one point in their history even passed a series of laws to counter its effects. They believed the most positive way of achieving this was to say something ridiculous or rude to the witch—indeed our habit today of 'touching wood' after describing one's present good fortune has derived from the Roman custom.

There can be little doubt, however, that people did on occasion, waste away and die after being overlooked, and medieval history is well larded with such accounts. Today we would explain it by the power of suggestion—applied with great cunning—and auto-hypnosis, but to the peasant mind then it was obviously the work of the Devil.

Cases of the evil eye are recorded up to recent times, and in Ireland belief in the evil eye still holds considerable sway. In Yorkshire, England, it is still held that a pear tree can be killed by a glance from someone with the 'eye,' and in certain farming areas in Europe instances of cows that go dry or milk that refuses to cream are attributed to overlooking.

'White' witches—those avowedly working only for good—have been much consulted to nullify the power of the evil eye, and one such person gave me a formula quite recently to effect a cure. The sufferer should first anoint the soles of his feet and the palms of his hands with a mixture of warm water and salt and then throw what is left of the fluid into the fire with a prayer for 'preservation from the eye of the devil.'

The fear of the evil eye has been recorded throughout history.

Possession

The condition of possession, whereby a person's body was 'invaded and taken over' by evil spirits who caused the sufferer to behave in strange ways, is another power attributed to witches. Demonologists in the Middle Ages declared that the witches had many ways of inflicting possession, but the easiest was to conceal a devil (specially conjured for the purpose) in an apple and then induce the chosen victim to eat it—spirit and all.

In France, Italy and England we find the most extensive records of possession. Nuns and small children were particularly prone, and their conditions varied from rolling on the floor screaming, to speaking in a strange voice (allegedly that of the devil or spirit who was possessing them) and vomiting the most unlikely objects (in one famous case in 1566 a group of Dutch children brought up needles, pieces of cloth, hair and even slivers of glass!).

In Spain and Italy, nuns in particular suffered from this affliction, and the Italian friar and scholar Francesco-Maria Guazzo wrote in the early seventeenth century that all those bound by vows of celibacy were particularly vulnerable and 'it was wonderful with what wiles the devil surrounded them to deter them from chastity.'

In France possession was said to have driven men and women to perversion, a view supported by Madeleine Bavent's 'confession,' published in 1652, in which she recorded priests and nuns indulging in homosexuality and lesbianism, and in bestiality and other obscene practices—all instigated by 'devils which had entered the souls of the good men and women.' An equally famous case is that which took place in the American village of Salem (see pages 104–105).

In England the most interesting occurrence of possession undoubtedly concerns one Thomas Darling, a 14-year-old who frequently developed convulsions after which he would accuse a local woman of having bewitched him. In 1596 he claimed to have had a vision of hell and seen devils torturing a group of witches. He also said he had seen an enormous chamber-pot from which flames were issuing!

Thomas Darling, one of the most famous cases of possession

Contortions indicated the first stage of demoniacal possession.

The doctor called to the boy diagnosed a case of worms, but the lad claimed he was harboring a devil and accused an old woman, Alice Gooderidge, of bewitching him. She was immediately seized and brought before the judiciary. With no more evidence than the wild claims of the boy, the trial got underway. On the second day matters took a further ludicrous turn when a notorious phony exorcist, John Darrell, presented himself in the court and said he would 'raise up and converse with' the devil in young Darling. Using his powers of ventriloquism he then conversed with the devil and, according to one report, 'by great wonder got the spirit to leave the child.'

All this hocus-pocus satisfied the judge, and the unfortunate old woman, hardly having been able to speak a word in her own defense, was committed to prison—where she died a few months later. Fortunately for justice—if not for the poor old lady—the case came in for a great deal of scrutiny by enlightened scholars, and a year later both Darling and the ventriloquist Darrell were exposed in a pamphlet prepared by Archbishop Samuel Harsnett.

Records show that there were many different ways of exorcizing an evil spirit. Whipping the sufferer's naked body to drive out the intruder was popular during the Middle Ages; this was superseded by prayer and the laying on of hands, a technique which has continued to the present day among certain holy orders. During the Middle Ages, too, the Church held special services of exorcism, often attended by large numbers of victims. They were lengthy affairs full of the most fervent exhortations to 'thee, most vile spirit' to leave the body.

Another popular form of treatment was a wheel-shaped instrument to which the afflicted person was attached and on which he was whirled around until 'the devils flew out in terror.' Contemporary illustrations often show small demons appearing from the mouths of those they had possessed and fleeing from the benedictions of priestly hands. These

One treatment for possession: the wheel designed to cast out devils

pictures, and the many lurid descriptions of objects allegedly vomited by sufferers, are presented in such a way that it is almost impossible to determine what the actual ailments were. But in the light of present medical knowledge there can be little doubt that many an illness which could not immediately be diagnosed was blamed on witchcraft and led to the persecution and death of some pathetic old crone.

Incubi and succubi

Apart from the familiars, imps, demons and spirits, there were still more sinister incubi and succubi—male and female devils respectively who sought sexual intercourse with humans. These two devils are recorded throughout Europe—particularly in warmer regions—and were apparently able to change their sex at a whim. Their main purpose, the demonologists tell us, was to prey on the sexual urges of men and women and win them over to the service of evil. As they could change their forms, travel through walls and control

An incubus as represented in Francis Barrett's *The Magus* (1801)

The pleasures of a demon lover: a 14th-century French manuscript

the willpower of those they sought to seduce, one can reasonably assume their task was not a difficult one.

Church authorities of the Middle Ages seem agreed that the incubi greatly outnumbered the succubi—because of 'women being more licentious than men.' What puzzled them more was whether children could result from these couplings. St. Thomas Aquinas, the most level-headed of commentators, wrote in the thirteenth century: 'If sometimes children are born from intercourse with demons, this is not because of the semen emitted by them, or from the bodies they have assumed, but through the semen taken from some man for this purpose.' The ways of collecting semen were most ingenious and ranged from stealing nocturnal emissions to forcible orgasm and the devil changing sex to receive the juices!

The most famous writer on this subject, the Italian Ludovico Maria Sinistrari, says in his *Demoniality,* written in the seventeenth century but not published in English until over one hundred years later, that the wiles employed by the incubi and succubi to seduce innocent victims 'were most cleverly devised to capture both the prize of virginity and the juices of life.'

When pursuing an unwilling victim, the spirits would assume the form of a trusted figure such as a father confessor or bishop (in the case of a girl) or a nun or some young and beautiful women of unimpeachable reputation (in the case of a man).

Several famous figures have been linked with these devils: Merlin, for instance, was reputedly fathered by an incubus, and Pope Sylvester II is supposed to have slept with a succubus throughout his rule as Father of the Catholic Church. In France, Italy and Spain we also find numerous records

Rarer than the incubus was its female equivalent, the succubus: 'a consequence of woman's greater appetites,' said the Churchmen.

of abbesses who cohabited with their incubi when allegedly at prayer in the confessional box.

From court records of witch trials we find plentiful evidencc that the accusation of intercourse with demons invariably meant that the guilty party was hustled off to the stake. The scantiest evidence seems to have been not only admissible but certain to lead to conviction. And in the late Middle Ages, husbands in certain European countries divorced their wives on the grounds that they slept with devils.

According to Sinistrari, men and women who willingly copulated with devils found all human love-making thereafter 'paltry and unable to arouse them by any degree.' He also recounts stories of strange monsters, half-human and half-beast, that resulted from the union of women and incubi.

Despite the mighty weight of evidence left by the Church authorities, it is a little difficult to believe that these devils were anything other than the results of erotic dreams or yet another excuse devised to cover illicit sexual intercourse. The charge that they were at the command of witches also seems completely without foundation.

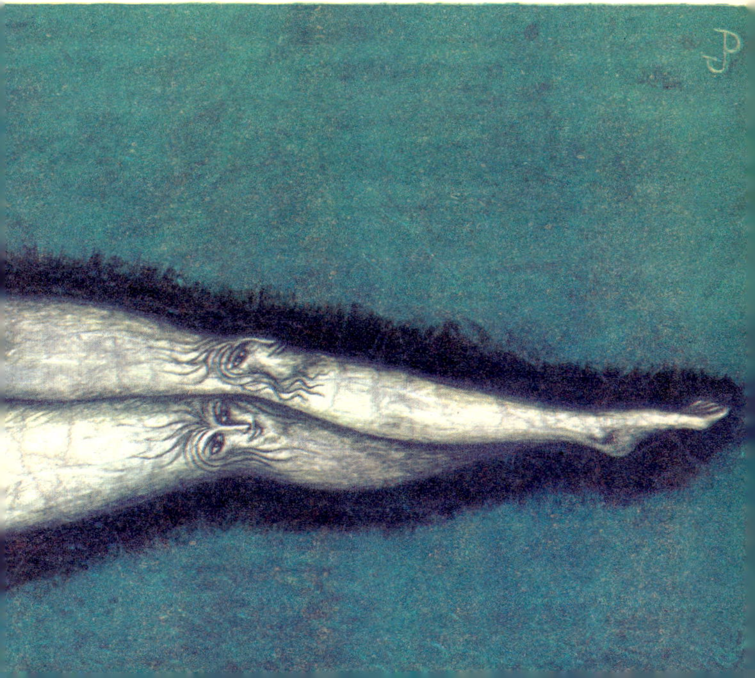

Saul learns his fate from the Witch of Endor, an early necromancer.

Necromancy

As we have seen, the art of necromancy, attempting to contact the dead, has been a part of witchcraft since earliest times. Although it has mostly been regarded as evil, some societies were more inclined to tolerate it if 'good angels and not devils were invoked for the purpose.'

In very ancient times necromancy was understood to be literally a descent into Hades to consult the dead, but it later came to be looked upon as the raising of a dead person's spirit to seek information about the future and the location of buried treasure. Probably the most famous instance in early history is the Old Testament story of Saul, who consulted the famous Witch of Endor about his forthcoming battle with the Philistines. Having seen the might of his enemy, the King sought vainly among his own advisers for guidance about the outcome of the conflict and then turned in desperation to the witch. She raised the spirit of a prophet who immediately foretold a total defeat for Saul. The King had unfortunately no alternative but to ride into battle and die alongside his soldiers.

More recent necromancers were reputed to have made pacts with the Devil for their knowledge and to have carried out their rites at midnight in deserted graveyards or ruined churches. They were also said to steal corpses needed for the ceremonies from local gibbets and 'could not be deterred from their evil missions by the authorities or the dead themselves.'

Necromantic manuscripts still in existence in certain European museums describe how the practitioner must prepare his magic circle by moonlight, recite the appropriate invocation and take great care to ensure that the spirit has departed before leaving the circle at the end of the ceremony 'or else risk being seized and carried to the netherworld of the dead.'

Many of necromancy's dark secrets still remain untold, and to study some of the terrible rites is to see why several authorities regard it as 'the most heinous sin and the form of witchcraft to be shunned above all others.'

Corpses stolen from the gibbet were much used by necromancers.

The Modern Merlin

There are no more important figures in the history of necromancy than Dr. John Dee and his assistant Edward Kelly, who practiced the art with considerable success during the reign of Queen Elizabeth I.

Dee, a brilliant scholar and mathematician, came across necromancy as a young man through the study of astronomy and dealings with certain famous European demonologists such as Johan Weyer and Jean Bodin. On his travels he had assembled one of the finest private collections of rare books on the dark arts ever recorded. Before he was befriended by the Queen, Dee earned a certain notoriety and was for a time imprisoned for being 'a companion of the hellhounds and a conjuror of wicked and damned spirits.' But at Elizabeth's court he became known as a 'Modern Merlin' and was much in demand for divining the future, using an oval mirror of obsidian through which he claimed to contact spirits.

In 1582 Dr. Dee met Kelly, a former apprentice to an apothecary and an undisguised rogue, who completely deceived the older man. In the years which followed, Kelly took the doctor in to the extent of making him believe he possessed a powder that could 'turn base metals into gold' and persuading him to indulge in wife-swapping, saying that a spirit had told him there should be 'the impartial using of matrimonial acts amongst any couple of us four.' (Needless to say Dr. Dee had at that time a young and beautiful wife who was also undoubtedly taken in by Kelly.)

Together the two men explored the realms of sorcery and necromancy. The authorities were not as gullible as Dr. Dee, however, and the younger man soon had to take himself off to Europe to avoid charges of fraud. He eventually died in Prague after trying to escape from a prison where he was being held to await trial for robbery and fraud.

Dee continued his work until his death in 1608 and, apart from developing a crystal ball (or 'shew stone') in which he foretold the wonders of the future for all,' he also published a pamphlet describing a conversation with an angel he claimed to have had through the art of necromancy.

Dr. John Dee and his notorious assistant, Edward Kelly

J. Dee E. Kelly

The crystal ball has played an important part in divination.

Divination

Divination, as distinct from necromancy, has always been used for good, and we have encountered its practice in our history several times. Divination by herbs, fire or special rods has always been popular, and the study of the entrails of animals is widely recorded in many civilizations. (This practice originated among primitive nomadic tribes, who used to examine the viscera of animals before picking a spot to camp, in order to discover if the neighborhood was healthy.) Each country developed its own styles of divination, and in the seventeenth century John Gaule in his remarkable study of the art lists no fewer than 50 different types.

The interpretation of dreams also comes within this category, and many a witch has been asked to divine what a strange nocturnal vision meant. In the Middle Ages numerous books and pamphlets on how to interpret dreams circulated, and some authorities claim that during this period almost every important event was announced to somebody by a dream.

The most famous story about divination concerns a Dr. Lamb who was the Duke of Buckingham's personal physician and deeply versed in alchemy and magic. Like so many witches of his kind, Dr. Lamb was greatly feared, and in 1640 a mob dragged him from his London house, chased him through the streets and finally stoned him to death at St. Paul's Cross.

But Dr. Lamb had entrusted many of his secrets to his housekeeper and mistress, Mrs. Anne Bodenham, and she capitalized on his notoriety by setting herself up as a wise woman. Her business flourished; there are several accounts of her 'drawing a circle upon the ground, throwing secret mixtures upon it and calling Beelzebub and his demons for advice.'

Despite her ever-growing list of clients, Mrs. Bodenham was destined for a similar end to that of Dr. Lamb. Ann Styles, a serving girl once employed by Mrs. Bodenham, was arrested for stealing silver and to save herself used the time-honored method of accusing her mistress of practicing witchcraft. She said Mrs. Bodenham could change into a black cat and had made her sign the 'Devil's book.'

A contemporary illustration of Anne Bodenham divining the future

The old woman was forthwith brought to trial, and two so-called witch's marks were found on her body. She was convicted and hanged in 1653—taking to the grave her own secrets and those of her strange master.

Sorcery

Sorcery, like divination, can be interpreted in various ways and figures prominently in the history of witchcraft. In its purest form it is an attempt to control nature and produce good or evil spirits.

In the Middle Ages, the Church defined sorcery as evoking demons to carry out those powers which 'God permitted to the Devil after He turned him out of Heaven,' whereas the practice of witchcraft was, in its eyes, the raising of spirits to 'commit acts against His ruling.' Of course this extraordinary distinction left the way open to all kinds of abuse, and we read of ludicrous instances where a man who had asked the Devil to help him seduce women was not guilty of affronting the Church, whereas a woman who resorted to the use of herbs in a desperate ritual to save her dying child was guilty—and hanged for her pains.

Nonetheless the practice of sorcery has continued through the ages and is still evident even today. In many countries one still finds the professed 'white' witch, usually an old peasant who can cure animals or reveal the future by employing this art. There are elements of sorcery, too, in the fortune-tellers who use pieces of hair or nail parings for their work—and indeed in all those who prey on the superstitious nature of man when selling charms or bracelets to ward off 'evil spirits and denizens of the other world.'

Like the witches, sorcerers have often been persecuted. In Europe in particular we read of numerous suspected sorcerers being burned alive in the fifteenth, sixteenth and seventeenth centuries. And quite recently in Italy, during a nine-month period there were five instances of peasants being sentenced to prison terms varying from three to five years for 'practicing the dark art of sorcery.'

The sorceress as seen in the 17th century, an interpretation of Vandervelt's famous print in the Bodleian Library, Oxford

The devil's mark

Records clearly demonstrate that one of the most damning pieces of 'evidence' that could be introduced during a witch trial was the devil's mark which the prosecutor would reveal on the accused's body.

Although the authorities often grouped them together, there were in fact two quite distinct marks supposedly given to show allegiance to evil—both equally explainable natural phenomena.

The devil's mark took the form of a scar or strip of oddly shaped dark skin, whereas the witch's mark was a piece of protruding flesh, or even a secondary pair of nipples, on which the witches' imps and familiars were supposed to feed. Both were allegedly awarded to the witch when initiated into the cult and sealed with sexual intercourse between Devil and neophyte.

The revealing of these marks was often done in the most degrading circumstances—women mostly being taken into

The devil's mark was alleged to be the seal of evil and the witch's mark an unnatural nipple: both are and were common aberrations.

public places, stripped, their bodies shaved of all hair and a mark revealed usually in the most intimate part of the body, the crotch. Some witch prosecutors also made doubly sure of a conviction by propounding the existence of an invisible devil's mark that could only be found by 'pricking.' Again the subject would be stripped and her or his body mercilessly jabbed with the special pricking instrument until a spot was found (or invented, see page 43) where no pain was felt or no blood flowed.

Today these marks—except those that were obviously self-imposed—would be dismissed as birthmarks, moles, warts or any other of the common small imperfections found on the body. But in the times of witch hysteria they were seen to have the shape of the Devil's cloven hoof, his finger-prints or even the imprint of his lips!

Again one cannot help remarking how ludicrous it is that these marks should have been looked upon for such a long time as suitable evidence for conviction of witchcraft. That they were not finally made inadmissable until the eighteenth century is a salutary indication of the extremes to which bigotry can drive us.

Levitation

The alleged ability of witches to fly and levitate has engrossed the minds of students of the occult through many ages. The great modern investigator of witchcraft and demonology, Montague Summers, wrote as short a while ago as 1946: 'It is very certain that witches can be, and are, levitated and so transported to the Sabbat.'

After our earlier mention of witch ointments and their hallucinatory powers (see page 67), this statement must be seriously questioned. However, Summers believes that the witch unguents had no power but that practitioners of the craft employed the same secret skills as the saints credited with the capacity for levitation.

'In the lives of the saints,' Summers writes in his *Witchcraft and Black Magic,* 'the phenomenon of levitation has been recorded again and again and the evidence is absolutely unimpeachable.' He goes on to quote the examples of St. Francis of Assisi, who was several times 'suspended above the earth, often to the height of three or four cubits,' and St. Gemma Galgani, a nun who lived at the end of the nineteenth century and was several times seen to be 'lifted into the air whilst she was entranced in prayer.'

Even in the very earliest records, witches are said to have been able to fly and their means of transport was either a broomstick or cleft stick. According to the *Medicatio Viri Incubo Divexati* published in 1645, the secret of flying was imparted to each witch after he or she had made the ritual vow of obedience.

Animals such as cats, goats and wolves were sometimes also employed for transportation and they, like the witches, had to be smeared in the witch ointment. According to the *Medicatio,* the main ingredient of this ointment was 'the fat of murdered children.'

Although records suggest that these were all safe and reliable means of going to and from the Sabbat, some authorities have noted that the sounding of church bells would cause 'the witch and her transport to fall from the skies.'

St. Francis of Assisi who, it was alleged, had been seen at certain times 'suspended above the earth to the height of several cubits'

The lycanthrope—a transition from human being to wolf

Werewolves

For much of history, lycanthrophy—the ability to change from human into wolf—has been readily accepted as another power of the witch. Classical writers as far back as Petronius have written of men and women who 'by night change their form to that of wolves and thereafter search for the flesh of humans.' Demonologists in other countries and at other times have added weight to the assertion that a physical change took place. They describe the growth of body hair, the walking on all fours and the reshaping of the head.

Several trials are recorded in medieval Germany in which the accused were said to have 'gone out at night in the shape of animals (wolves) and seized and devoured the bodies of old men and babies.'

Apparently potions had to be taken before the transformation could proceed, and it was necessary to drink them while stripped naked and wearing the skin of a wolf in a moonlit clearing. To return to human form was simplicity itself: the werewolf merely had to urinate.

Several cultures also record people who possessed 'werewolf tendencies' and, while not changing shape, did from time to time growl, run about on their hands and knees and mutilate the bodies of children, eating their flesh and drinking their blood. In our more enlightened times we would see mental derangement here rather than service to the Devil.

The wounding of wolves and the subsequent discovery of similar injuries on humans—some kind of sympathetic process—has also figured largely in the tales of lycanthropy. Jean de Nynauld in his *De La Lycanthropie* (1615) tells of a woodman who cut off the leg of a wolf which immediately turned into a woman lacking an arm.

The most famous trial of a lycanthrope was that of Peter Stubb at Cologne in 1589. Stubb confessed that by means of a magic belt he was transformed into a 'greedy, devouring wolf' and committed many murders. To return to his normal form, he said, he merely had to remove the belt. Stubb's plea for mercy on the grounds that it was witchcraft which had forced him into these acts was overruled and he was savagely put to death by having his skin peeled from his body, his limbs broken and his corpse finally burned to ashes.

Vampires

'They are the bodies of deceased persons, animated by evil spirits, which come out of the graves in the nighttime, suck the blood of many of the living, and thereby destroy them.' Such was the description of a vampire given in an English broadsheet in 1734.

Like the werewolf, the vampire has been associated with witchcraft, and it, too, has a special place in literature. The word itself comes from the Hungarian, although some scholars suspect it may be of even older origin, coming possibly from the Turkish word for witch.

The vampire emerged on the occult scene in the West at quite a late date, however, and there are few reports of it before the end of the seventeenth century. Nevertheless it was a creature held in great fear because of its need for regular supplies of fresh blood.

The souls who became vampires were said to be suicides and criminals, whose bodies, according to tradition, did not decompose in the grave until their allotted timespan was complete. They rose up on certain nights and sought sleeping victims from whom they would draw blood using their fanged teeth. After this they could lie in suspended animation for months, even years, on end.

In the same way that witches were 'revealed' by marks and teats, so were vampires said to be those with 'harelips, hair on the palms of their hands, blue eyes and red hair.'

Germany has suffered more than any other country from vampires and many treatises exist in that language setting forth the explanation of, and cure for, their attentions. All countries are, in fact, agreed that human vampires can be killed only by discovering the grave from which they come and driving a stake through their hearts.

Of late the colorful novels and films about vampires—in particular, Bram Stoker's *Dracula*—have lent almost enchantment to a 'monster' who was possibly some kind of disturbed person, rendered outcast by a morbid craving for blood.

The strange figure of the vampire has been a focus of superstition since the 17th century and still engages popular interest today.

The literature of witchcraft

No study of this kind would be complete without reference to the famous books, or *grimoires,* of witchcraft. Records show that a great many books on the occult are now lost to us, but a number of works remain which help our understanding of the darker sides of witchcraft, necromancy and sorcery.

Probably the most remarkable of all is the *Devil's Bible,* seized by the Swedes in Prague in 1648 and now in the Royal Library in Stockholm. The book is taller than a man, contains 300 parchment pages each the size of a double-bed sheet, and is bound in oak planks 1½ inches thick. According to legend it was the work of a monk arrested for practicing the dark arts and offered his freedom if he could write down in one night all the secrets of his craft. He apparently did so—calling on the Devil himself to help.

The very earliest books on witchcraft date back to Roman times and, apart from instructions on how to raise spirits for both good and evil, are much filled with prophecy and divination. Many early books are rumored to exist or have existed. Ancient ceremonials were mostly never recorded, and forgeries of supposedly authentic works are common. Reliable data are therefore hard to find.

Another famous work that is still obtainable is *Les Secrets Admirables du Grand Albert,* supposedly the work of a Dominican Bishop of Cologne, St. Alban the Great, who died in 1280. It is a handbook for all who would practice 'black' magic and is full of obscene rites and ceremonies. It has a 'twin' in *Le Petit Albert* (The Rare and Cabbalistic Secrets of Albert the Less), the work of one Alberto Lucio Minore, which deals almost exclusively with necromancy. Also still in existence is *The Greater Key of Solomon the King,* which dates from the fourteenth or fifteenth century and is alleged to have been composed in Hebrew. It tells how to conjure spirits, become invisible, find treasure and generally make life easier for the owner!

The work most widely derided by authorities—yet most closely secreted—is *Le Grand Grimoire* 'on how to trick and deceive the Devil into your service without cost to your

The monk of Prague and his master at work on the *Devil's Bible*

soul.' There are probably fewer than half a dozen handwritten copies in the world—all unavailable for inspection.

On the other hand, of course, there are the books, reports and pamphlets which attack witchcraft and direct 'how it should be put down and those who practice it punished unto death.' Most famous of all is the notorious *Malleus Maleficarum* (see pages 30–31), the witch hunter's apologia.

Almost as important is Reginald Scot's *Discovery of Witchcraft* published in 1584, certainly the first work in English on witchcraft. Scot was horrified by the mass executions of witches and believed the 'witchcraft epidemic' was nothing more than a scare started by the Inquisition to cover its wholesale butchery. Hailed in some quarters for its common sense, the work was damned by the Church and the authorities, and when James I became King of England in 1603, all the copies that could be found were burned. There are several other notable works in English which brought

The cover of a contemporary tract on the Witch of Newbury (1643)

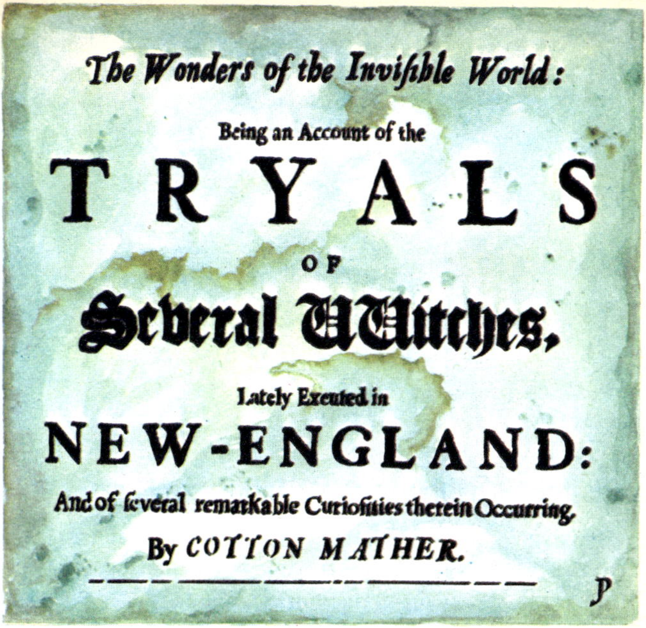

The title page of colonial America's most famous witchcraft book (1693)

rationality to the topic, in particular Archbishop Samuel Harsnett's *Discovery of the Fraudulent Practices of John Darrell* (1599), *Saducismus Triumphatus* by Joseph Glanville (1681) and John Wagstaffe's *Question of Witchcraft Debated* (1669). For the forces of unreason there were the *Demonology* of King James and *Wonders of the Invisible World* (1693) by the American witch hunter, Cotton Mather (see page 104).

Pamphlets and broadsheets detailing the witch trials were also very popular and sold cheaply in enormous quantities throughout Europe. Museums hold quite a number of these publications and from them we get evocative, if not very accurate, descriptions of the trials in prose and verse. Pamphleteers (often publishing at their own expense) wielded considerable power, and, unhindered by the laws of libel, could attack and condemn as they pleased. Many an old scold found herself hauled up before a court on charges set against her in a pamphlet—and once in print the accusations had a habit of sticking.

Famous witch trials

In a popular history of witchcraft such as this it is obviously not possible to devote more than a few pages to the witch trials, although in fact their number and interest value are great. We shall look, then, at four particularly famous cases. Together they span almost 250 years, and they show that reactions to the 'noxious heresy' were almost uniform during this period.

The accusations made against some peasants at **Arras** in northern France in 1459 constitute one of the very earliest charges of witchcraft on record. And, as was so often the case, the denunciation was made by a suspect witness (on this occasion a condemned prisoner). Indicted stood a feeble-minded old woman, Deniselle Grenières, four other women and an old painter, Jehan la Vitte, said to be leader of the coven.

The old woman was summarily tortured by the inquisitor, Pierre le Broussart, and said all six had met with the Devil, worshiped him, partaken of a feast and then copulated indiscriminately. To avoid similar treatment, la Vitte tried to cut his tongue out but only succeeded in badly cutting his mouth. After all six had made statements under torture, these were reviewed by theological experts who found there was no direct affront to the Church intended, nor any murder and crime involved, and recommended the Inquisition to have mercy. The advice was not taken, however, and on May 6, 1460 the group were dressed in the 'uniform' of heretics—a garment decorated with evil spirits and a miter portraying the Devil—exhibited before the local populace and then burned alive, struggling and screaming their innocence to the end.

But the affair did not end there. Pierre le Broussart continued his inquiries and in succeeding months brought a whole procession of other men and women to torture and trial. Rich and poor alike suffered at his hands—but the wealthy did at least have a last-minute opportunity of buying back their lives if they could afford le Broussart's price.

The six alleged witches who were exhibited in the 'uniforms of heretics' and burned at the stake in Arras, France, in 1460

However, terrible reports of the persecution at Arras began to spread throughout France, and in 1461 the Parliament in Paris intervened, investigated the circumstances and announced that the Inquisition had not only exceeded its brief but executed many innocent people. It was scant satisfaction to the dead, but almost without exception all those who had gone to the stake were later exonerated by Parliament.

In England the first important witch trial took place in the Essex market town of **Chelmsford** in 1566, hard on the heels of Queen Elizabeth's Witchcraft Act of 1563. The accused were three women from the small village of Hatfield Peverel, just outside Chelmsford. The first, Elizabeth Francis, was accused of bewitching a child; the second, an old widow, Agnes Waterhouse, of bewitching and murder; and the third, Mrs. Waterhouse's 18-year-old daughter Joan, was charged with attempting to bewitch the chief witness against her mother.

All three women were said in court to be well versed in

The 'thing like a black dog' mentioned in the first Chelmsford trial

Victims of the third Chelmsford trial (1589): a contemporary print

the 'dark arts' and Elizabeth Francis was alleged to have given her familiar to Mother Waterhouse. This familiar, in the shape of a cat, was called 'Sathan' and apparently had the ability to turn itself into a toad. It had also instructed Elizabeth how to win herself a husband by seduction.

Mrs. Waterhouse, it was claimed, had used the familiar to 'kill with a bloody flux' a man with whom she had quarreled. This statement was quickly accepted and the poor woman was summarily sentenced and dispatched to the scaffold – the first woman in modern England to be hung for witchcraft.

In the case against the younger Waterhouse, a 12-year-old child said Joan had sent 'a thing like a black dog with a face like an ape and a pair of horns' to bewitch her and prevent her testifying. However, discrepancies were found in the story and Joan was freed – along with Elizabeth Francis whose case was also found not proved.

As at Arras, this was not to be the end of the affair. A decade later, four more women from the district were tried on similar charges—one of them being Elizabeth Francis. This time she, with two of the others, was found guilty and hanged. Three more witch trials also took place in the town, the first involving a group of 14 women from St. Osyth and the third being brought in 1645 by the notorious witch finder, Matthew Hopkins. In this case some 32 people were accused, of whom 19 were hung and the rest imprisoned—all on the highly suspect evidence of a few small children; it has rightly gone down as the most terrible witch trial in English history.

The witch trial at **Eichstätt** in Germany in 1637 is as rich as any in descriptions of Sabbats, night riding, orgies and necromancy. Yet, like the other two cases we have considered, it was colored by the words of a poor, deluded old woman tortured to the verge of madness and in the end believing herself capable of any vileness. Contemporary records do not name this woman but report that she had apparently lived with her husband and eight children for over 20 years before being accused of being a witch.

On the opening day of her trial she 'laughed heartily' at the charges and said she preferred death to admitting she

was in league with the Devil. Her determination obviously unnerved the magistrates for they immediately began searching for a witch's mark and allegedly found one on her shoulder. Torture followed and after a session on the notorious 'stretching ladder' the old woman admitted that the Devil had come to her about 18 years before—in the shape of a hangman! She immediately fell in love with him and was prepared to do his bidding. The Master of Evil named her 'Shinterin' (Bone Breaker) and gave her some powders and ointment which she could use to transport herself to the Sabbat and cause evil to her enemies. He later commanded her to use it on her husband to quieten him when he came to her and also to kill one of her children 'in obedience to his wishes.'

After further torture the unfortunate old woman confessed to more killings, the practice of necromancy and even to having had visits from the Devil while she was in prison. In her delirium she also named 45 other villagers as accomplices. Three weeks to the day from the opening of her trial the old woman died as a result of her treatment. She had admitted to everything proposed to her by the

The 'stretching ladder' was used in the brutal Eichstätt trial.

magistrates and in fact by her words had let loose in the district of Eichstätt a persecution which in the following years was to bring over 400 men and women to execution.

The witch trial that took place in 1692 at the little settlement of **Salem** is the most famous in American history. This alleged outbreak of witchcraft occurred in the rigidly Puritan area of New England where hell-fire was held to be a reality and the Devil an adversary who had to be fought with the severest possible measures. The people of Salem, primarily of English stock, believed implicitly in the existence of witches and their ability to 'possess' souls for the Devil's cause.

The case has been so well documented that we need note it only in outline. The 'outbreak' began in the home of the local minister, Reverend Samuel Parris, when some small children were reported to have been seized by fits and convulsions. When questioned, the children accused three people of bewitching them: the Parris family's old West Indian servant and two aged village women. The trial was conducted in the European manner, for word of such trials had spread far and wide in the American colonies. The old women were induced to confess to all manner of dealings in evil and to indict friends and neighbors for similar practices.

In a very short space of time, trials and persecution spread throughout New England with the same speed and malicious intent as in Europe. At the center of this frenzied activity was Cotton Mather, a narrow-minded High Churchman with Matthew Hopkins's brand of zeal. Mather wrote a report on the Salem outbreak, *Wonders of the Invisible World* (1693); 'an account of the sufferings brought upon the country by witchcraft,' it is still available today and clearly shows the workings of prejudice and ignorance at their worst.

However, in time people came to see how unfairly their superstitions had been exploited, and Mather's power declined. Many of his supporters turned against him, making him the major scapegoat for a reign of terror which had condemned a great many innocent people to death.

Colonial America's chief crusader against the evils of witchcraft

COTTON
MATHER

The Loudun nuns

Monks and nuns have figured prominently in the history of witchcraft, but nowhere with more notoriety than in the Loudun case in 1633, where priest and nuns combined in the extraordinary tale of an entire convent apparently bewitched by demons!

The man at the center of the affair was the parish priest of Loudun, Father Urbain Grandier. He was already notorious throughout the area for having seduced the daughter of a public prosecutor and taken as his mistress one of the young girls who came to him for confession (a common practice in western Europe!). It was alleged that he had sent two demons, Asmodeus and Zabulon, to take possession of the nuns and cause them to have severe fits.

At his trial it was stated that devil's marks had been found on Grandier's body when he had been searched, and a copy of a pact he had made with the Devil discovered among his possessions (see pages 64–65). Statements were read by 60

A sketch made at the time of the burning of Urbain Grandier (1634)

A portrait of Father Grandier from ecclesiastical records

witnesses who 'deposed to adulteries, sacrileges, and other crimes, committed by the accused, even in the most secret places of the church.'

As the trial progressed, however, a number of the nuns tried to withdraw their statements, saying they had been told to 'confess' by certain of Grandier's powerful enemies. The defendant had stated his innocence right from the outset and maintained this even under severe torture.

Nonetheless the forces of 'law and order' won and Grandier was burned alive—convicted on the grounds that 'every time he prayed to God he was in fact evoking the Devil.' It was small consolation to the Father (who did undoubtedly practice certain dark rites) but several of his main accusers died in the ensuing months of mysterious illnesses. The nuns, too, continued to suffer from convulsions—turning Loudun into something of an attraction for the curious!

Black Magic

Great confusion has existed about the terms witchcraft, Black Magic and the Black Mass. So far we have considered only witchcraft, seeing how it has developed from an ancient fertility religion and suffered greatly from persecution and an almost total failure on most people's part to approach the subject rationally. We have, of course, seen that it does contain 'black' elements: the Sabbat and its supposed ritual obedience to the Devil, the conjuring of demons to work evil and the opportunity for sexual promiscuity can hardly be looked upon as less than sinister. But there is not, until the sixteenth century, concrete evidence to support the existence of true Black Magic—a ritual devised and carried out to affront and parody Christianity and demonstrate the believer's dedication to the perpetration of evil.

A. E. Waite underlines this point in *The Antiquity of Magic Rituals*: 'Each of the occult sciences was, however, liable to that species of abuse which is technically known as Black Magic . . . White Magic is an attempt to communicate with Good Spirits for a good, or at least innocent, purpose. Black Magic is an attempt to deny God and communicate with Evil Spirits for an evil purpose.'

The creation of the actual Black Magic ritual ceremony, or Black Mass, was primarily the handiwork of Catherine de Medici (1519–89), wife of Henry II of France and instigator of the St. Bartholemew Day massacre. Always a woman of licentious and depraved tastes, she was drawn to the darker elements of the occult, then very widespread in Europe. After the death of her husband in 1559, she gathered around her a select group of courtiers to experiment with the dark arts and soon devised a ceremony in which a blasphemous mass (that of the Catholic Church read backward) was said over the naked body of a girl and followed by a sex orgy.

Catherine was soon introducing the delights of the Black Mass to people in high places throughout the country (thus obtaining political control as well), and this was to have far-reaching effects both at home and abroad in the centuries to come.

Catherine de Medici (1519–89), creator of the Black Mass

Black Magic practitioners

As so often happens, what became fashionable in France spread rapidly throughout the capitals of Europe, and we soon read of Black Masses modeled on those of Catherine de Medici being conducted in Germany, Austria, Spain and Italy. In England, too, we find the ceremony being 'performed by certain debased gentry and their ladies'; searching for new sensations by bored nobles was often the motive for dabbling in Black Magic.

And it was not long before the common people took up the idea and began to use certain elements of Black Magic. In France we read that the devil-worshiping King Henry III was himself the subject of an intensive murder campaign by a group of black magicians. They met regularly in a clearing outside Paris and thrust knives into an effigy of the King, afterward urinating on it. However, it was a fanatic who eventually assassinated him in 1589.

Records throughout Europe point to the fact that there were quite a large number of renegade and defrocked priests involved in Black Magic, and their inventiveness is sometimes little short of amazing. The Abbé Becarelli, for instance, highlighted the ceremonies he conducted by handing out small lozenges which were supposed to cause the recipients to change sex! And from the Basque region of France came the Mass of St. Secaire, in which water taken from a well where an unbaptized child had been drowned was used in a death spell.

Not surprisingly a great many unwanted children were born as a result of these infamous masses—children who could recognize no father and were unwanted by the mothers. If we believe contemporary gossip, some of them were sacrificed at the masses as the ultimate affront to Christian teaching—but because of their numbers, special organizations were set up to dispose of the infants with the least possible fuss. A Frenchwoman nicknamed La Voisin organized such a 'disposal service' and her exposure triggered off the Chambre Ardente Affair, one of the most horrifying stories of the period.

France's Black Magic monarch: Henry III, practitioner and victim

The Chambre Ardente Affair

Even in retrospect, the events which culminated in the revelations of the Chambre Ardente are truly fantastic. We read of venerable Catholic priests cutting the throats of newborn babies over the bodies of naked women . . . of noblemen and their wives poisoning or killing their families and relatives 'in obedience to evil' . . . and one of the King's mistresses endeavoring to regain his affections by blood sacrifice and debasement.

The story begins with the arrest of one Catherine Deshayes, widely known as La Voisin and ostensibly a fortuneteller, who was accused with others of arranging the disposal of unwanted children and supplying poisons to be used for the removal of troublesome third parties. Because of the nature of the crimes, the King himself agreed that a special tribunal should be set up and proceed with its inquiries in secrecy. It was also to meet in a room draped in black and lit with candles—hence the name *la chambre ardente*.

For nearly a year, confession after confession was extracted from La Voisin and her accomplices, and a steadily increasing procession of marquises and their ladies and mistresses was brought before the tribunal to testify. A horrifying picture began to emerge—debauched ceremonies enacted throughout Europe, widespread poisoning and dedication to evil—and the affair culminated in the revelation that a former mistress of the King, Madame de Montespan, had conducted Black Masses in order to win back Louis's love or kill him and his latest mistress.

At this point the tribunal, who were reporting regularly to the King, were ordered to continue in even greater secrecy. And told that under no circumstances were more of the French nobility to be questioned—despite the fact that it was now obvious the whole Black Magic network emanated from Madame de Montespan and *abbés* and dignitaries who moved in the highest circles. After a while even the pretence of further inquiries was stopped and the practitioners were free to continue their obscene rites as they pleased.

The human altar has been a constant feature of Black Magic. Add infanticide and the horror of the Chambre Ardente Affair is apparent.

S
W

LONGFELLOW

The spread of Black Magic

The Chambre Ardente Affair spotlighted what was happening in France. Elsewhere in Europe we find similar reports of ceremonies where blood sacrifices were made, young girls raped and defiled, churches attacked and outraged, and debauchery found fresh depths to plumb in the search for new evils. To a certain extent this was a backwash from the Protestant Reformation, which brought all church rules into question.

Several historians have recorded how men and women steeped in Black Magic would attend church, receive the sacrament at mass, and then carry it away for defilement and blasphemy at their ceremonies. They have rightly observed that these people never sought to raise the Devil in person—in fact they did not believe in his existence *per se*—but used him as a personification of the evil they glorified.

There are stories, too, of Black Magic bibles bound in human skin being used in Germany, candles made from the fat of children in Spain and Italy, and in England a variety of instruments of flagellation to add 'spice' to the ceremonies.

In *Là Bas*, Joris-Karl Huysmans, the French historian and novelist, describes how he learned at a Black Mass in a deserted chapel that 'the devil's service is honored in most countries in the world.' He got even more specific information about the New World and was told that in the American colonies there was 'a whole society of Black Magicians under the direction of a Scotsman named Longfellow' (not the poet!). Huysmans noted that certain individuals were now 'most concerned' about the rise in devil worship and were plotting to expose those who 'practice such evil blasphemies, particularly those who enjoy positions of trust and authority as they are the most dangerous threat to our society.'

So, as we have seen, Black Magic with its infamous Black Mass was firmly, though discreetly, entrenched in society. We shall see later how it has lasted to this day, merely changing some of its concepts to adapt to fluctuating social conditions, but not altering in the slightest its basic premise of promoting evil by sexual perversion and reviling the Christian Church.

Longfellow, the famous American society figure and black magician

MODERN WITCHCRAFT AND BLACK MAGIC

Persecution continues

As we saw at the end of the first section, English authorities regarded the repeal of the Witchcraft Act in 1736 as a declaration that the Old Religion was finally dead. This, of course, was nonsense and all the Act could be said to have achieved was protection for practicing witches in the courts of law against indiscriminate prosecution and biased conviction. For understanding of the craft it did very little.

Indeed the majority of the population in England and elsewhere still clung to its superstitious fears of 'witch powers,' on occasions meting out its own rough justice when the authorities would not take the action it demanded. Too often the authorities turned a blind eye to these occurrences. Records show us, in fact, that the number of witches being 'swum' or otherwise ill-treated hardly decreased at all. In 1737, for instance, a witch was 'swum' three times in England, and when the villagers were still not satisfied of her

A suspected witch being 'swum'—an illustration from a 17th-century pamphlet, *Witches Apprehended, Examined and Executed*

innocence she was weighed against the church bible (this being another test for witchcraft) and, outweighing it, was judged guilty.

Many of the clergy, too, continued to campaign against the craft and one dedicated priest in Leicestershire, England, the Reverend Joseph Juxon, even delivered a special sermon 'occasioned by the late attempt to discover witches by swimming' in which he revived all the old fears.

Also in England, in 1751 the 'swimming' of John and Ruth Osborne, who were said to have destroyed a farmer's stock and made him 'ill with a strange sickness,' led to the death of the old couple. Not long afterward in Northampton, England, Sarah Bradshaw, accused of practicing witchcraft, actually volunteered to undergo the swimming test to prove her innocence. She apparently plunged to the bottom of the village pond and when she spluttered to the surface some minutes later was judged 'not guilty.' Even today her courage, in the face both of possible drowning and prejudice which could quite easily have refuted all signs of innocence, is remarkable.

But there was nothing unique about the slowness of the dawn of enlightenment in England; throughout Europe the picture is much the same.

In France, the practice of witchcraft had ceased to be held as a crime after the burning of a warlock in Bordeaux in 1718, but in outlying villages, fear still engendered hostility against old crones. The same was true in Spain and Italy, while in Poland in 1750 a village mayor turned a blind eye when his people burned alive two men who 'sang the Devil's name and called curses on the district.'

In Germany, however, the practice of witchcraft was a capital crime long after most other countries had repealed such legislation. The last trial and execution of a European witch took place in Bavaria as late as 1775. The unfortunate victim was a serving girl, Anna Maria Schwägel, who was seduced by a young coachman—on his own admission 'a trafficer with devils'—and joined him at local Sabbats. She renounced her Catholic faith at his request and would probably have happily continued thus if she had not suddenly discovered he was married. In fear and bitter anger Anna Maria fled the district and was eventually found begging and half-demented in the streets of Kempten. She was put into a home and there confessed her secret life to other inmates, who immediately informed the matron.

In the ensuing trial she confessed that it was 'the Devil in the form of a coachman who betrayed me.' The magistrates, however, were more inclined to believe that the young man had been the Grand Master of a coven of devil worshipers and had seduced her to 'increase his evil flock of devil sheep.' They judged her subsequent complicity inexcusable and the extreme punishment of German law, beheading, was imposed on her. It is a salutary thought that if these affairs had come to light just a few years later, the worst Anna Maria might have expected would have been a reprimand from the justices and some earnest prayers for her soul from a priest.

The last witch to suffer the death penalty in Europe—in 1775

Anna Maria
Schwägel

The Buxen, a band of German Satanists who terrorized the country

The Satanists

Throughout the period in which the witchcraft acts were being repealed and people were slowly working persecution out of their hearts, the Old Religion itself went through a change. Once more the devotees began to group together and the idea of the coven was again more widely accepted. New members were not easily recruited, however, and for the next two centuries the numbers of people practicing the craft can at best be described as meager.

In examining the latter half of the eighteenth century in Europe, we also find the rise of a new kind of underground devil-worshiping cult, the Satanists. They differed only slightly from the black magicians, for although they intended no direct attack on the Church, they were nonetheless equally dedicated to evil and obscenity. Such cults drew their members from all strata of society and visualized Satan as a kind of invisible Grand Master of their order.

Typical of these were the German Buxen, a band of men and women led by several noblemen, who roamed the countryside at night dressed in cloaks and death's head masks. Whole districts lived in fear of these people, who would stop where they chose, practice their Black Mass and necromancy in front of terrified hostages and then disappear into the night. They were not above bloodshed and rape, so the authorities were much hampered in their attempts to capture members by the villagers' fear of reprisals if they talked.

The Buxen — and other organizations like it — was also very fond of using live animals in its sacrificial rites, and signs of its passing were found not only in Germany, but also France, Italy and Austria. One cult of Satanists in northern France even seized a young peasant girl, conducted a ceremony over her naked body and then left her with a wave of their masks — too quick and alert for the authorities who plodded on their trail.

These cults were in many respects the forerunners of today's devil worshipers. Their mobility, their open practicing of the dark arts and their obvious contempt for the law are all elements in twentieth-century Black Magic.

Satanists robbing fresh graves for ceremonial victims

The Hell-Fire Club
In England, as in all of Europe, the Satanists flourished, and we read of a host of cults with evil and debauchery as their purpose—cults with extraordinary names like 'Sons of Midnight,' 'The Mohocks,' 'The Banditti' and 'The Blasters.' The young bucks of the eighteenth century, always on the lookout for new ways to prove their manhood and daring, were particularly attracted to them, but many of their elders were also lured by the promise of orgy and perversion held out in return for the trifling promise of obedience to evil.

Most famous of all was the 'Hell-Fire Club,' sometimes known as 'The Monks of Medmenham' and founded by Sir Francis Dashwood. Although there were several other hell-fire clubs in Britain—Ireland had a particularly strong one led by the miniaturist Peter Lens—the cult based at West Wycombe on Sir Francis's vast country estate was the most notorious. At 16, the young lord had inherited a great deal of land and wealth and in the style of the time immediately set about discovering to what depths of depravity he could plumb. He furnished his mansion with obscene frescoes and statues and decided to practice Satanism in the ruins of Medmenham Abbey, which stood in his grounds.

His interest in devil worship had stemmed from being initiated into a cult while touring on the European continent, and he brought back from his travels a great many rare and diabolical *grimoires*. He had Medmenham fitted with 'cells' where his brother members—or 'monks' as they were soon calling themselves—could retire to enjoy the prostitutes who had been brought in for the main ceremonial.

In its time the Hell-Fire Club included in its ranks some of the most distinguished aristocracy and men of the arts in the land, and their individual power and rank was such that opposition to their activities stood little chance of success. However, internal dissent and jaded palates eventually brought an end to the activities of the Monks of Medmenham. The ruins of the Abbey stand to this day, and a thriving tourist industry is based on stories of what happened at the meetings of the Hell-Fire Club.

Orgy and blasphemy were the keynote of the Monks of Medmenham.

The Black Magic hoax

Although it was to be a great many years before Satanism threw up a figure as important as Sir Francis Dashwood, the practice continued through the remainder of the eighteenth and then the nineteenth century. And in 1877, Dr. Charles Hacks was writing: 'Throughout the world Satan is being worshiped more devoutly and on a greater scale than ever before.' We read of Satanists performing a ceremony coupling a male and female ape on an alter in Calcutta; in London white lambs were sacrificed across the naked bodies of young girls and then torn limb from limb by the faithful; in Vienna a satanic circle tortured an investigator to death and then escaped justice because one member was a senior law official.

But of all these incidents, the most famous one of the period concerns the book of confessions written by a certain Diana Vaughan, allegedly at the heart of devil worship in France. In the work, *Memoirs of an ex-Palladist,* Diana described a network of female Satanists spread throughout Europe who allowed male members but structured the rites very much to their own needs. She told of how she and her companions, the Palladists, performed bestial acts of adoration to Satan and looked for the day when they might overthrow the accepted morals of society.

She also described her change of heart, saying that one morning she was striken with remorse over her terrible ways and vowed to seek the sanctuary of the Church. On its publication the book caused a furor throughout Europe; despite the fact that no one was allowed to see or meet Diana Vaughan (she was in retreat to clear her soul, said her publishers) her story was believed—to what extent can be judged by the fact that two important bishops ordered special prayers and a mass to be said for the luckless girl.

But the bubble burst—the whole story was a hoax. Diana Vaughan and her cult were fiction, the creation of a talented French journalist and occult investigator, Gabriel Jogand. If nothing else, however, the book demonstrated in one stroke how narrow was the dividing line between fact and fiction in Satanism.

'Diana Vaughan,' so-called exposer of Black Magic in France

DIANA VAUGHAN

Aleister Crowley

In the annals of modern Black Magic there has been no more notorious practitioner than the Englishman Aleister Crowley, or 'The Great Beast,' as he called himself. The international press also had its own succint title for him: 'The Wickedest Man In The World.'

Although since his death the extent of Crowley's involvement with Satanism and Black Magic has been much debated, there can be little doubt that a man who openly admitted to practicing animal sacrifice (the first such occasion being when he was 12 with a tiny kitten), torture, drug-taking, obscene nude rituals and the composition of works encouraging 'evil for evil's sake' was more on the side of the Devil than Christianity.

Crowley was a man of brilliant scholarship and considerable courage. (He led a party to climb Mount Kilimanjaro while still a college student.) His search for the 'truth about man and the dark arts' began in 1898 when he joined the Hermetic Order of the Golden Dawn, then the most important occult society in the English-speaking world, with members like W. B. Yeats, Arthur Machen and Dion Fortune. Its secret rituals became too tame for him and at the turn of the century he withdrew to begin his own experiments at a secluded mansion at Boleskine, close to Loch Ness.

In the months that followed his arrival, rumors were rife in the nearby village of strange noises and of devil worship being practiced at the mansion. Crowley was unperturbed by gossip and indeed hit back at it with his own brand of persecution—causing two servants to commit suicide, a butcher who received one of his checks covered with demonic names and signs to sever an artery while cutting meat, and a harmless parish worker to turn into a hopeless alcoholic. Finally tiring of the quiet life at Boleskine and having perfected many of the rituals of evil on which he had been working, Crowley set out on a world tour to find disciples for his new order of black magicians.

He studied extensively in Egypt and the United States,

Aleister Crowley, the most important figure in 20th-century occultism, who practiced Black Magic and 'evil for evil's sake' where he wrote a detailed report of how he had parodied the Crucifixion using a toad as the Messiah. He was also intent on sexual conquest and perversion and could already boast a great many successes; no doubt his shaven head and magnetic eyes had an almost hypnotic power over women.

At this time his basic philosophy could be summarized in the single sentence which he delighted in repeating in speech and letters: 'Do what thou wilt shall be the whole of the law.' He was also delighting in awarding himself new titles after he progressed farther into evil ('Brother Perdurabo' and 'The Master Theron' being just two) and humiliating his various mistresses—all of whom he referred to as 'my scarlet women'—by forcing them to take part in orgies at which they became 'The Ape of Thoth' or 'The Dog.'

As the number of his disciples grew, Crowley decided to establish a permanent base on the island of Cefalu, just off the coast of Sicily. There, in a mountainside villa which he called the Abbey of Thelema, he conducted continual Black Magic

A Black Mass was performed at Crowley's funeral in 1944.

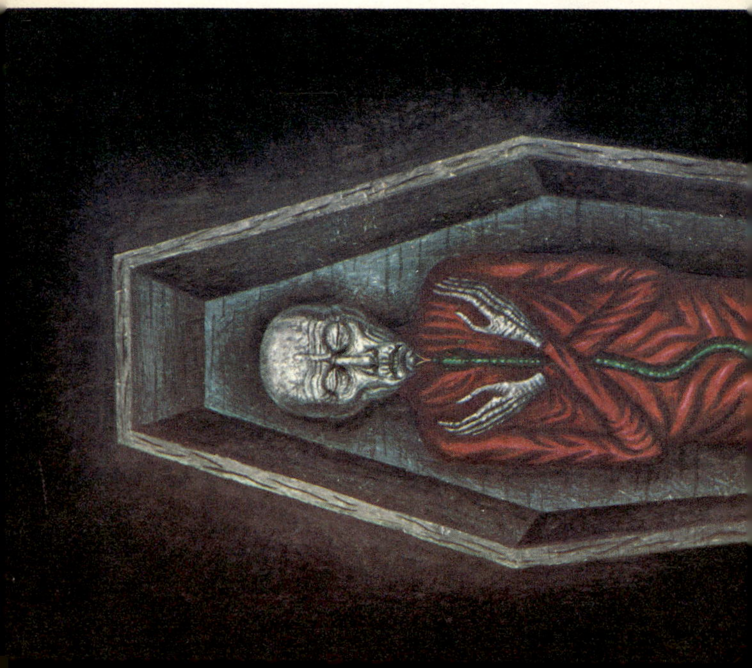

rituals, sacrifices and orgies—all dedicated to glorifying evil. He wrote extensively, too, describing his satanic rites, the ways to achieve closer harmony with perfect evil and endless details of his day-to-day life.

But remote as the Abbey was, it did not entirely escape the attention of the authorities, and, when in 1923 it was rumored that a baby had been stolen from a nearby village and sacrificed by Crowley, expulsion was inevitable. The little group returned to England where 'The Master' began publication of his work and his followers commenced the propagation of his ideal of 'evil for evil's sake.'

Aleister Crowley died in 1944, his body wasted by drugs and his mind corrupted by the evil he had seen and perpetrated. But his influence did not die with him—his work had helped reshape Satanism and Black Magic into patterns appropriate for the twentieth century. Those who laughed at the news that a form of Black Mass had been conducted at his funeral would have been less ready to smirk if they had known of the desecration, obscenity and perversion that were to follow as a result of 'The Great Beast's' work.

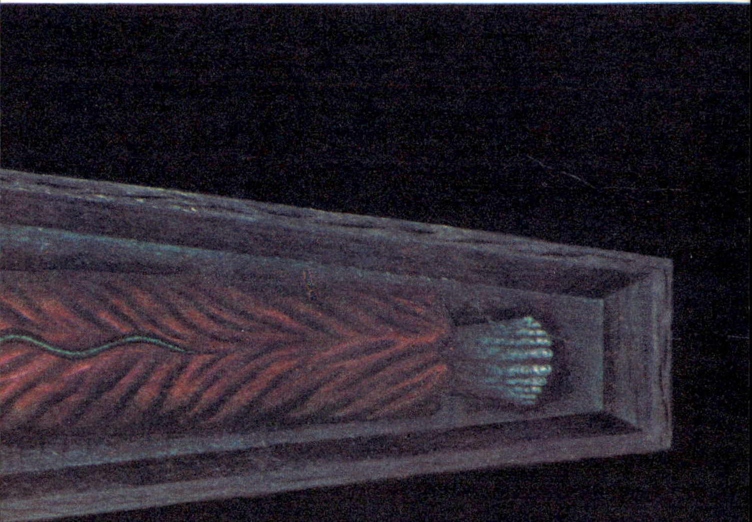

Satanism and the Nazis

Before we turn to the major figure in modern witchcraft we should not overlook a small, but fascinating, sidelight—the relationship between Satanism and the Nazi Party. In the 1930's a number of students of the occult—notably the Englishman, Lewis Spence—were warning that in their opinion there were satanic elements in Nazi Germany which, when unleashed, could 'enslave the world in evil.' While not actually accusing the Fatherland's leaders of practicing devil worship, Spence for one said that Adolf Hitler was enthralled by his country's long history of consorting with evil and the powers which supposedly could be engendered. He summarized his beliefs: 'It is evident that Hitler's mentality is under the influence of the Satanist power from his vacillations, his lack of self-control, his epileptoid seizures of rage and the spirit in which he has dealt with the people who have fallen into his hands.'

Now we know that the Fuehrer and those closest to him were deeply interested in spiritualism and fortune telling (indeed Hitler had his own astrologer). But the claims which certain authorities (not Lewis Spence) have advanced that Nazi leaders actually took part in Black Magic rituals—burning effigies of their opponents and sacrificing animals—are perhaps just a little too outlandish to credit.

Author Dennis Wheatley, whose novels on Black Magic are highly regarded for their obvious knowledge of the occult, has also been much intrigued by the suggestion that strange supernatural powers were at work in Nazi Germany; in fact he used this idea in one of his most remarkable tales, *They Used Dark Forces,* the story of a plot to kill Hitler by satanic rites! He has commented on the subject: 'Although we know Satanism and Devil Worship were practiced in Germany during the years of the war, I have found no evidence that Hitler or those closest to him were involved.'

Probably we shall never solve this puzzle, but because of Germany's long association with the supernatural one cannot dismiss the possibility that the Nazis employed Satanism.

Satanism and occult rituals were rumored in the Third Reich.

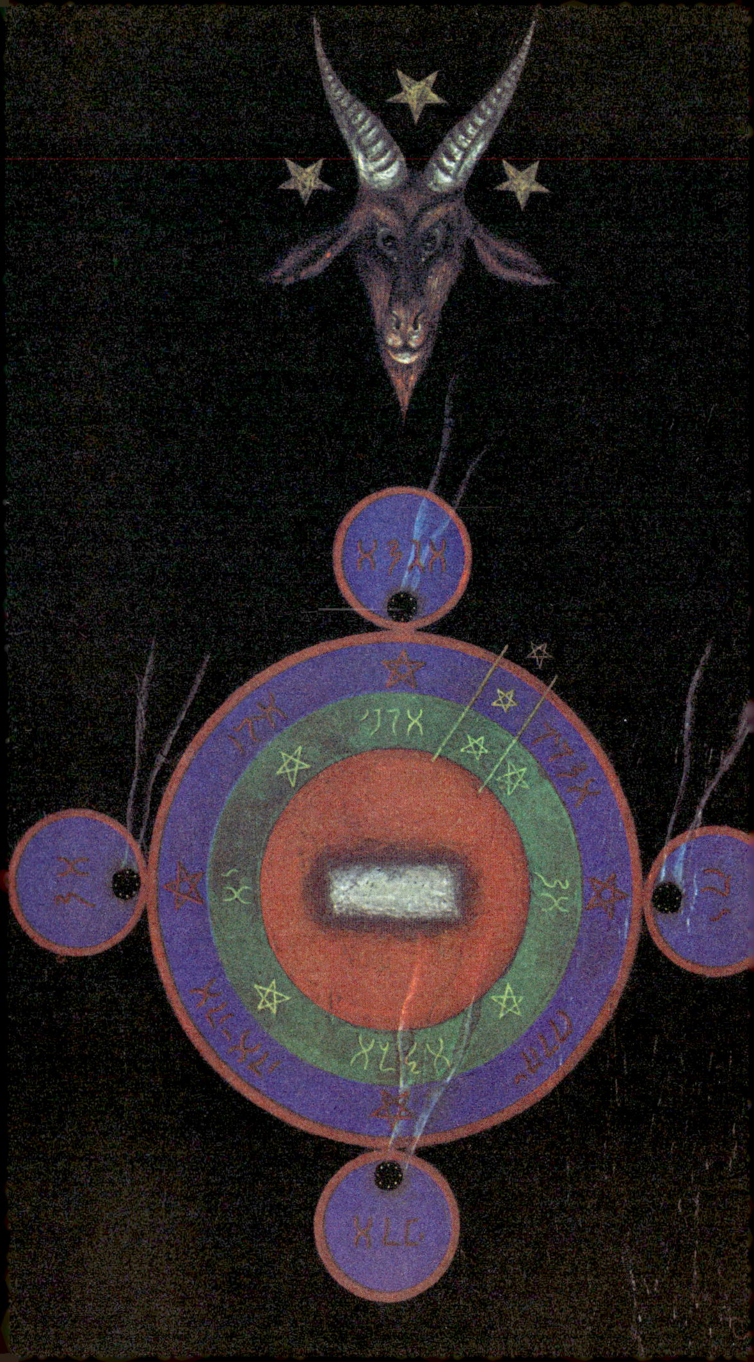

Modern witchcraft

As Aleister Crowley neared the end of his life, having successfully spearheaded the practice of 'evil for evil's sake,' a former associate of his in the Golden Dawn, Dr. Gerald Brosseau Gardner, was deeply involved in restructuring the Old Religion to suit the twentieth century.

Dr. Gardner (his doctorates were in philosophy and literature) spent his working life in Malaya but used his spare time to research into the occult; when he returned to England in 1946 to retire, he was the possessor of a formidable knowledge of ancient religions. He chose to settle on the Isle of Man and soon surprised the local populace by opening a witchcraft museum in an old mill that had reputedly been used by witches for many centuries.

Having been a practicing witch for many years, he felt the craft needed more application to modern life and redevised the basic rites and ceremonies. Support came quickly and his followers multiplied throughout the British Isles. Covens sprang up from one end of the country to the other, and Dr. Gardner was kept busy traveling from one group to another, initiating and explaining.

Helped greatly by the common-sense explanation of witchcraft given in Dr. Murray's *The Witch Cult in Western Europe,* Dr. Gardner saw a gradual change in public opinion. 'Harmless cranks with a taste for nudity' was an early, and to him, almost acceptable assessment after the centuries of brutal persecution. Then in 1951, the repeal of the Witchcraft Act completely removed the possibility of prosecution for practicing *wicca.*

Not all the changes that Dr. Gardner introduced into the craft have been accepted, and today there are certain covens that deny his importance in witchcraft. Nonetheless he gave witches a new confidence and the courage to propound their faith in public. When he died in 1964, he left behind a flourishing craft with a membership of several thousand and ritual observances that successfully linked the witches of the twentieth century with their earliest ancestors.

An exact copy of the modern witchcraft ceremonial circle as drawn by Gerald Gardner. The goat's head indicates the north.

The rites of witchcraft

The witchcraft ceremony of reverence to the Old Gods (The Great Mother and the Horned God), while basically the same throughout the world, is probably more 'refined' and carefully observed in Britain, so for this reason we shall examine a ceremony conducted in London rather than one in a city in the United States or elsewhere.

Secrecy is still, as one might expect, of importance to the witches and therefore the rituals are usually conducted behind closed curtains in an anonymous suburban house or in some remote wood or on a hillside. (Also one has to remember that nudity, an important part of the observance, might well be said by the authorities to cause a breach of the peace if observed by outsiders, and the witches are not eager to be the subject of more legal proceedings.)

Very little equipment is needed for the ceremony, the most important items being an altar made from a tressel table covered with a white cloth and around it a consecrated circle nine feet

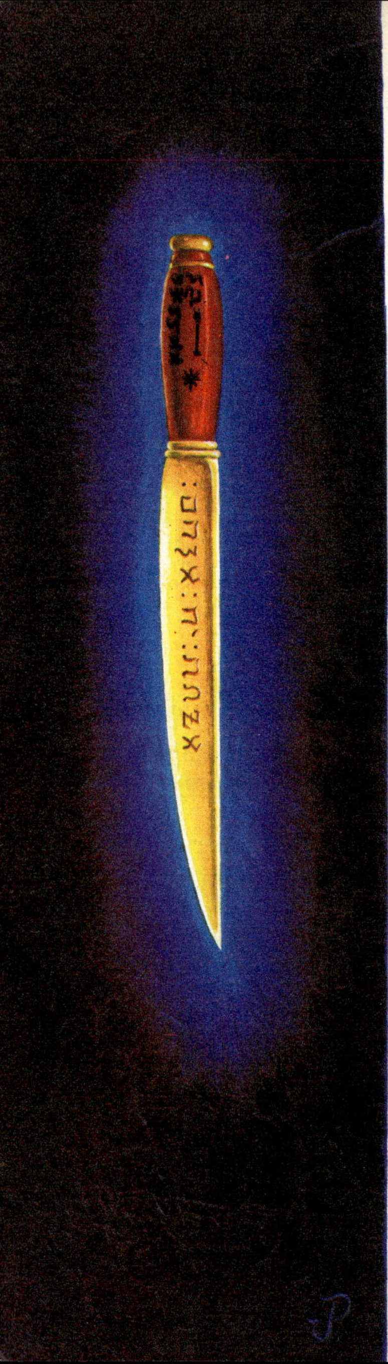

The *athame*, or ritual knife

in diameter marked on the floor in chalk or tape. Around the circle are the cabbalistic symbols of the craft, which are designed to help conjure up the power of the Gods. Four candles are placed just outside the circle to denote the points of the compass, and on the altar itself is a censer (containing burning incense), a whip or scourge, the *athame* (a small knife), a copper pentacle, a long-bladed sword and containers of salt and water.

The ceremony itself can be conducted by either a high priest or priestess: the woman representing the goddess of fertility, The Great Mother, and the man—wearing a bronze helmet with a horn on each side—the Horned or Hunting God. They may be naked or clothed in white robes. Usually when a man officiates a female member of the coven assists him as a symbolic 'Mother.' To reach the position of leadership in most serious covens today a person has to be a member of the craft for at least three years and prove himself 'devoted, honest and true.'

When all is ready the

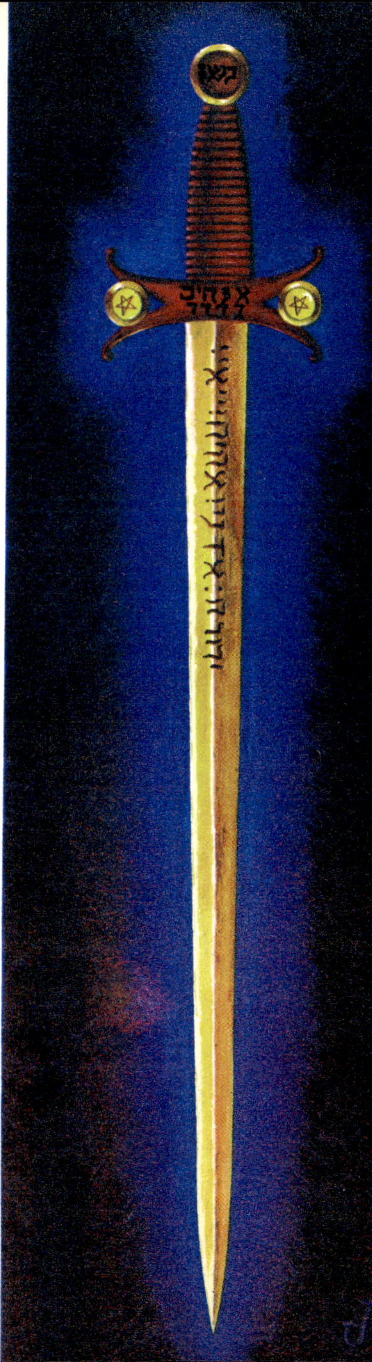

The ceremonial sword

High Priest will call the 12 worshipers together, using their witch names (such as Lilith or Tanith) and they place themselves around the circumference of the circle. All must be naked, for the witches believe that clothes 'stifle the bodily emanations' that help them raise the forces of good.

The litany for the rites is taken from a large tome, *The Book of Shadows,* which lies on a stand beside the altar. The text of the book is of considerable age, and after initiation each new high priest or priestess is allowed to make a copy by hand for his or her own use.

The *wicca* ceremony is divided into four parts: the blessing of the coven, the ritual dance, the initiation of a new member (if applicable) and the request to the Gods on behalf of the faithful.

The magic circle is first consecrated with salt and water and the High Priest recites over the bowed heads of the witches the ancient prayer: 'Eko, Eko, Azarak, Eko, Eko, Zamelak, Eko, Eko, Eko, Eko!'

Then the ceremonial circle is formed—by the witches linking hands. They dance around the magic circle slowly, and at the appropriate moment the High Priest calls: 'I summon and call you, Mighty Ones of the North, East, South and West, to witness our rites and guard our people.' Background music is sometimes played at this point to 'help the swing' of the dancing and the High Priest will also gently scourge the members with the whip, 'driving out unclean spirits.'

If a new witch is to be admitted to the coven, the due ceremony will take place now, the neophyte standing naked at a point immediately in front of the altar. Raising high the *athame,* the High Priest turns to the east and informs the Gods that another initiate is to enter their ranks and calls for blessing.

The neophyte is now allowed to enter the consecrated circle—by a specially prepared gap—and stands before the altar. He is then blindfolded and his wrists bound behind his back with a cord which is also tied around his neck. In some

The High Priest of a modern witch coven begins the ceremony of worship with an invocation to the Old Gods.

covens the initiate is also covered with a white sheet that is later pulled off to symbolize rebirth into *wicca*. He is next informed by the High Priest of the new life he is entering and warned not to pass on any of the secrets he will learn to others. This he must swear, and he seals his promise with his blood, making a small cut on his finger.

At the climax of the ceremony the ritual sword is placed against the disciple's breast and he is required to vow obedience to the cult 'on his life.' (As witches believe in reincarnation he may also be threatened with losing his chance of life after death if he is not faithful to the craft 'in every manner of working.') This completed, the High Priest unties the blindfold and cord and gives the required 'five-fold kiss' on the feet, knees, sexual organs, breast and lips of the neophyte to signify a new witch is born.

After a pause in which the new witch joins his companions around the circle, the High Priest asks the Gods for the gift of health and prosperity for the men and well-being and

A neophyte, bound with cord, undergoes ritual admission to the witch cult—at sword-point and commanded by a high priestess

fertility for the women. More dancing invariably concludes the gathering—and while no student of the occult, and witchcraft in particular, would deny that the highly charged and emotional atmosphere in which the naked witches work has sometimes led to intercourse between consenting members, this is considered the exception, not the rule.

When a witch becomes a high priest or priestess, a similar ritual is observed—with a more intimate contact made between initiate and initiator and a resolve sworn to keep closely all the great secrets of *wicca* and 'return good with good threefold.' Occasionally, too, a spell may be cast to cure illness or relieve anxiety and the formula for this will come from one of a group of ancient prayers.

This much of 'white' witchcraft remains standard throughout the world, and it is on the evidence of ceremonies like this that the witches ask for understanding and an end to the stories of unspeakable orgies and degradation which have for so long bedeviled them and their craft. However, one must point out that—human nature being what it is—the secrets of advanced witchcraft are doubtless used in some circles for lust and perversion.

Superstition dies hard

The twentieth century has seen a radical change in public attitudes toward many previous taboos, but witchcraft has had to wait until the middle of the century—and the permissive society—before finding real understanding among thinking people. Even so, police and newspaper records show that suspicious villagers in many outlying areas in Europe were still brutally attacking those suspected of witchcraft well into the middle years of this century.

Superstition certainly dies hard. In Mexico in 1935, for instance, law officers were tipped off just too late to prevent villagers from burning to death five old women accused of casting spells and 'conjuring up the fiend.' In France, too, there have been reports of peasants 'swimming' suspected witches across the Loire, and in England, in the 'Witch County' of Essex, the practice was almost a regular occurrence until the late 1930's. The story is still told there of a poor old man in his nineties, a self-professed witch and wise man nicknamed 'Dummy,' who made his living by selling charrns and spells and died from shock after being thrown into a pond at Sible Hedingham by one dissatisfied customer.

In Norfolk, England a witch hunt of some size developed in 1940 when a 'witch's ladder'—a long cord tied in elaborate strands and interwoven with the feathers of a black hen—was found in the belfry of a church. This was considered to be an attempt to 'spell' the church and its congregation, and the local constabulary had to be on the alert during the ensuing weeks when the homes of a number of old men and women were visited by a group of self-professed witch finders.

In contrast to this is the extraordinary event that took place in the United States during World War II which shows witchcraft not only being allowed to take place by the authorities, but by implication encouraged! A group of professed witches dressed in white ceremonial robes met regularly in a public park in Washington, D.C., to 'lay a curse on Hitler' by sticking pins into his effigy and reciting a prayer of evil. At the end of the war one of the group proudly claimed Germany had been overthrown by occult means!

'Dummy,' a recent victim of prejudice and superstition

Genuine practitioners of the old religion of *wicca* have not had their cause helped by the recent sacrilege and desecration.

Witchcraft into the open

Following the repeal of the Witchcraft Act in 1951, British witches—and later their brothers and sisters elsewhere—felt an urge to try for the first time to explain their craft to the public and perhaps after the centuries of persecution gain a measure of understanding.

The first step was the interviewing on radio and television of the high priests and priestesses of several covens, who showed themselves—no doubt to the surprise of many—to be ordinary men and women, living in typical suburban homes and doing perfectly normal jobs. They convincingly explained their craft, its history and their 'good intentions.'

A large group of self-professed witches earned newspaper headlines when they confronted a learned historian delivering a lecture in London entitled 'Witchcraft—a Myth' and demanded an apology. Then came the first Witchcraft Information Center, created to advise the public on the real aims and achievements of *wicca*. The chief liaison officer, matron of an old people's home, still runs the service today.

However, the witches' case has not been helped by the much-publicized outbreak in recent years of church and cemetery desecrations; almost without exception, these have been labeled by the news media as the work of witchcraft practitioners. It began in earnest in 1963 with the discovery of a violated grave at the derelict, hilltop church of St. Mary's in Bedfordshire, England; bones had been removed from the grave and used in some secret ceremony. The trail of reports continues unbroken to the present day—the figures climbing yearly. In the United States and Europe, too, animal hearts pierced with thorns, crude wax images stuck with pins and church buildings obscenely defiled have been reported and give rise to increasing concern.

Opponents of witchcraft have not been slow to seize on these outbreaks, but it is possible to state with some certainty that the vast majority are the work of children, perverts or fledgling black magicians carrying out their pledge to defile Christianity. Of course the genuine witches are not surprised at being blamed—it is not the first time they have been made a scapegoat. But they do abhor these occurrences because they are extremely damaging to their case for being a harmless religion practicing only good.

Modern Black Magic

Black Magic . . . Satanism . . . devil worship—the practice of 'evil for evil's sake' lives on in the twentieth century, thanks to the reshaping it received at the hands of Aleister Crowley and the inherent evil in man which can be all too easily unleashed.

Today's black magicians certainly do not believe in the Devil as a person to be summoned from the bowels of the earth, nor do they hold rituals to conjure demons and spirits. Instead, Black Magic today is directed toward sensual pleasures, the undermining of society and its morals and the corruption of the young.

Those who belong to these cults of degradation meet regularly, frequently holding a Black Mass parodying the Christian Mass and then indulging in the vilest kinds of carnality and perversion. They affront religion and society by their desecration of holy buildings and cemeteries, corrupt those who will not willingly join their ranks by intimidation and blackmail and have undoubtedly infiltrated into many strata of our social business life.

Reports of their activities are not plentiful—the threats held out to any who might wish to leave their ranks or reveal their secrets are many and severe—but of their existence and purpose there can be no doubt.

Dennis Wheatley has written: 'Satanism is an evil, living force in our midst and I certainly believe it is highly dangerous for anyone to become involved with these people, however much of a lark it might at first seem.' Churchmen, civic leaders and policemen all echo these words and at least two newspapers in Britain have campaigned determinedly against this 'cancer in our society.'

There is little point in elaborating further on the obscenities of Black Magic and Satanism in a popular history such as this. Suffice it to say then that no popularization of the subjects in films, on television or in books should ever be allowed to belie the underlying evil and degeneracy of the pursuits.

To judge from gruesome contemporary events, the power of modern Black Magic is embracing all kinds of people and enslaving them in its chains of evil.

Voodoo

The emergence of the independent nations in Africa and the immigration of black people into many European nations have spotlighted the black man's version of witchcraft. In the Americas it is usually known as *conjur* or *voodoo.* The Haitian version of voodoo, or *voudun,* is probably the most elaborate and best studied, but similar practices are known in Brazil, Trinidad, Jamaica, Cuba and the United States. These practices developed among the African slaves shipped to the Caribbean as sugar plantation workers in the seventeenth century. To the African gods brought over by the slaves, were added elements of Catholic ritual—and in some cases Protestant hymns—copied from their new masters. The result is a new blend, differing in detail from island to island and in the various geographic locations where black people live. But in all, there is a shared belief in possession, blood sacrifice and the use of drums.

Houngans (male) and *mambos* (female) share the role of priests. Apart from being able to cure sickness, they are also credited with the ability to inflict injury or death, reanimate the dead as *zombies* and influence individual lives by means of charms and spells.

The first really accurate account of voodoo ceremonies was written by a Frenchman, Moreau de Saint-Mery, in the early 1800's. He describes ceremonies as always being held by a priest surrounded by the magic circle, which also contains an altar. A snake representing the spirit Damballa is kept in a box on the altar, and the female priest, or *mambo,* sits on this box. When the spirit takes possession of her, she speaks oracles. That some form of 'possession' takes place has been substantiated by many observers; it has also been photographed. The underlying reason for this phenomenon, however, is still very much a mystery. Sacrifices of goats and cockerels are commonly made, and the blood is then used to 'seal the lips of the worshipers.' Drums add to the excitement of the ceremonies and are sometimes believed to contain 'souls' or spirits. However, not all drumming is

Voodoo continues to hold sway over its followers however far they travel. This is an interpretation of its powerful priestesses.

MAMBO

sacred, as drum rhythms are also used in stimulating the cooperative work parties that play such a large part in Caribbean life. When the voodoo ceremony reaches a high pitch, the dancing participants fall into a state of psychic intoxication, during which they can juggle with white-hot irons, dance in flames, eat broken glass and stir boiling water with their hands, without apparent pain or after-effects.

Most of the voodoo rites have been traced to Dahomey by modern anthropologists, but other versions can be attributed to tribes linked with the Congo or the Niger delta. Common to all of them is a firm belief that images containing some personal elements, such as nails or hair, can be used to cause injury, and that soul and body can be separated with dire results to their owner.

As in Europe, some practitioners of voodoo have turned their knowledge into methods of obtaining power, personal satisfaction and wealth. The late dictator of Haiti, Dr. François 'Papa Doc' Duvalier, was reputed to be the top *houngan* of the cult. Cases of outrageous fees demanded for removing

The pagan deities or *loa* are represented by a snake in the voodoo rites. Much of the cult's symbolism relates to the sacred serpent.

spells crop up occasionally in newspapers in the United States and Europe. In addition, tourists and travelers have published lurid tales of sexual orgies, ritual murders and stories about the living dead, or *zombies,* few of which can be checked for their factual basis.

Recently some of the same blend of European Christianity, African belief and mixed witchcraft practices has been making progress in the newly independent nations of Africa. Some of them have self-proclaimed popes or prophets, but almost all of them depend on their followers believing in the power of spells and ceremonies to promote well-being, wealth and sexual prowess. The more extreme versions of Satanism seem to reappear in some of the secret societies of Africa, the Mau-Mau, the Leopard Society and others. There have been reports of ritual cannibalism, and opponents of the societies and their leaders have been found brutally murdered. Some of the secret society leaders have also claimed the power to protect their followers from being hurt by knives or bullets, but the sexual excesses of Europe find little echo in Africa.

The situation today

Few readers, confronted by such a weight of evidence, will deny the continuing existence of both witchcraft and Black Magic. Both, however, can be seen in different guises in different parts of the world, and to conclude this short history we shall look at some examples. First, witchcraft.

In Germany, the country to have suffered most extensively from witch persecution, there are still approximately 70 cases of alleged witchcraft brought before the West German courts each year to be judged under the laws relating to fraud. (The Communist sector appears not to suffer from such occurrences—or at least they are not recorded.) In a recent interesting case a farmer in the small village of Berg called in a local witch finder after his cows dried up and four calves died. The finder decided that the farmer's wife was responsible and she was forthwith confined in a small attic and fed on dog food. Finally she became so emaciated the farmer was forced to call in a doctor for fear she might die. Terrified to disclose what had happened, the woman took enough treatment to regain her strength and then fled to her parents' home. Later she filed divorce proceedings and repeated her story in court. However, the witch finder, who had been the cause of all the trouble, was not even questioned.

In Kenya, in Africa, a number of witch doctors have been causing trouble for the authorities at soccer matches. They have apparently been running along the touchlines at games and casting spells on their team's opponents. When teams found themselves being outplayed they suspected it was because the ball had been bewitched and demanded that the referee change it. One referee highlighted the problem when he said: 'Something must be done—you can't impose a penalty simply because a player complains he's been bewitched!'

In Australia, scientists have been investigating the power of Aboriginal witch doctors who can 'sing to death' those who displease them. Recently, for the first time on record, doctors were able to save someone 'spelled' in this way—a boy who came upon tribal witches at a secret ceremony. In

Based on many authenticated accounts, there can be no doubt that the fear of witchcraft and Black Magic continues to envelop parts of the world today.

the past, Aborigines have invariably gone into a coma and died after this chanted curse. But in the recent case, the boy, hardly breathing, was rushed to an oxygen tent in Darwin.

In war-torn Africa, witchcraft has often been noted by correspondents. Congolese soldiers in particular have been seen running unprotected into fusillades of enemy fire, convinced that potions prepared by their witch doctors and rubbed on their bodies will give them immunity. Many of these men belong to the cult of Dhawa, which avoids all contact with white people, believes in 'black' magic and forbids concourse with women. One army commander facing these troops has said: 'They take no cover and chant and wave their weapons as they approach. If they suffer a defeat it is said to be because their witchcraft was not strong enough – but they rise again on the third day.'

In Scotland *wicca* cults are again thriving and some have even begun advertising for new recruits in the personal

Congolese soldiers charge into battle, believing themselves immune to all injury through the protection of 'black' magic.

columns of certain magazines. In one journal recently an Edinburgh firm was offering track suits to witch covens 'to be worn when the weather is inclement.' A Scottish witch also told me that her mail had suddenly started to swell with requests for flying ointments and do-it-yourself Black Magic kits. She added: 'I have also been asked for the secret of how to turn people into frogs and whether I could put my correspondents in touch with vampires and werewolves!'

While there are obviously still a great many people who treat witchcraft as a huge joke, the number seriously pursuing its ideals has much increased. A recent estimate suggested that in Britain alone there are now some 10,000 practicing witches, and in the United States the numbers are said to be much larger.

I know from personal experience that witchcraft is flourishing in the United States. Young people in particular are very eager to join the numerous covens which can be found from New York to Los Angeles and Detroit to New Orleans. According to one authority, there is a flourishing coven in Hollywood, led by a former movie actress, and in Boston there are no fewer than thirteen. In Los Angeles the authorities have shown what must amount to the most amazing public acceptance of witchcraft in all history—they have appointed a Mrs. Louise Huebner as Official County Witch to 'lend a little magic to public entertainment.'

The American witches have adopted their own passwords, 'Perfect Trust and Perfect Love,' but address each other with the same kind of ancient names as their colleagues in Europe. And instead of describing themselves as being 'naked' at their ceremonies they say they are 'skyclad.'

The most famous witch in the United States is Mrs. Sybil Leek, an English clairvoyant who came here some years ago to lecture and stayed. The daughter of a witch, she was initiated into *wicca* as a young girl and for many years lived in a rambling house in the New Forest in England, quietly leading her own coven and writing on the occult. Her charm and obvious sincerity have won her many admirers but she has resisted all the financial lures of 'going commercial.' She recently wrote of witchcraft: 'The United States has a few established covens but 50 times as many pseudo ones as anywhere else in the world. However, we are seeing more and more genuine covens being established all over the world and there is no doubt in my mind that it will not be long before witchcraft is accepted as a valid religion to take its place alongside all the others—free at last of persecution and fear.'

One of Britain's most recent and widely publicized witchcraft personalities is Alex Sanders, a dark, intense man who claims to be 'King of the Witches' and head of 107 covens. Sanders says he is the most powerful witch in Europe and in attempting to prove this has allowed film and television cameras into the most secret of his rites and ceremonies. As yet it is too early to determine his importance to the craft.

And what, in conclusion, of Black Magic and Satanism?

In the part of England in which I live, there have quite recently been reports of the Black Mass being observed. A 'white' witch I know told me: 'There are some very strange people here and to probe their activities too deeply would be like lifting the lid of Pandora's box.'

I have learned of devil worshipers at work in most areas of Britain, particularly around large towns, and throughout the rest of Europe, with Paris, Vienna and Rome as focal points. In Sicily recently a woman was imprisoned for killing her husband, who she claimed was a black magician. She said he had forced her to take part in degraded blood sacrifices, recruit young girls for his pleasure and help him invoke devils. Finally, in a terrifying ceremony 'when [she] felt a tidal wave of evil in the room' she turned the knife on her husband instead of the sacrificial chicken.

The use of Black Magic powers for seduction is also reported and I have newspaper cuttings from the United States, England and France recounting stories of young girls who claim that men have subjected them to 'evil influences' in order to have intercourse. In two of the cases the men involved actually boasted of being Satanists, and in the third the man had the goat's head symbol of Lucifer tatooed on his chest. (The use of hypnotism would probably explain most of these cases.)

Unquestionably the most extraordinary figure in Satanism today is Anton Szandor LaVey, a former circus artist, who has founded the 'First Church of Satan' in San Francisco.

Three important figures in the modern occult scene in the United States: (*left to right*) Louise Huebner, Anton Szandor LaVey and Sybil Leek

LaVey calls himself 'The Black Pope' and the successor to Aleister Crowley's position in the hierarchy of Black Magic. His principal aims are to glorify all carnal pleasures—'to sin is to fulfill yourself'—and reestablish the idea of Satan as a deity for worship. His disciples meet regularly to perform the Black Mass he has devised and take lessons from the Master's work, the *Satanic Bible*. Already they conduct their own baptisms, weddings and funerals—mostly employing the body of a naked girl as the altar and heavily attended by press photographers—and claim to be establishing new churches in other parts of the United States as well as England, France, Germany, Africa and Australia.

Sinister or a kind of weird 'black' joke? In our anything-goes society it may not be easy to decide. But in the case of genuine Black Magic, which courts no publicity, we can have little doubt of its evil influence—or that it is still often practiced in many countries of the world.

BOOKS TO READ

Complete Book of Witch Craft by Rollo Ahmed. Paperback Library, 1970.

World of the Witches by Julio C. Baroja. University of Chicago Press, 1965.

Witchcraft from the Inside by Raymond B. Buckland. Llewellyn Publications, 1970.

Witchcraft Today by Gerald B. Gardner. Citadel Press, 1970.

Magic, White and Black by Franz Hartman. Universal Books, 1970.

Witchcraft by Pennethorne Hughes. Penguin, 1970.

Mastering Witchcraft: A Practical Guide for Witches, Warlocks and Covens by Paul Huson. Putnam, 1970.

Aradia, the Gospel of the Witches by Charles G. Leland. Llewellyn Publications.

Witchcraft and Demonianism by C. H. L'Estrange-Ewen. Barnes and Noble, 1970.

Witches: Investigating an Ancient Religion by Thomas C. Lethbridge. Humanities, 1962.

Dark World of Witches: the Story of Witchcraft from the Beginning to the Present Day by Eric Maple. Pegasus, 1970.

The Witch Cult in Western Europe by Margaret Murray. Oxford Univ. Press, 1921.

Geography of Witchcraft by Montague Summers. Universal Books, 1958.

History of Witchcraft by Montague Summers. Citadel Press, 1970.

Voodoo: the Living Gods of Haiti by Maya Deren. Random House, 1970.

Some earlier books:

Discoverie of Witchcraft by Reginald Scot. Reprinted by Centaur, Southern Illinois Univ. Press, 1964.

Letters on Demonology and Witchcraft by Sir Walter Scott. Reprinted by Taplinger, 1970.

Malleus Maleficarum by J. Kramer and H. Sprenger. Reprinted by The Hogarth Press, 1928.

Saducismus Triumphatus by Joseph Glanville. Reprinted by Schol. Facsimiles, 1966.

INDEX

Add to your KNOWLEDGE THROUGH COLOR

(All Books $1.45 Each)
(Where marked ⓒ $1.95 Each)

The opposite page lists the currently available and constantly growing books in this new paperback series. To add to your KNOWLEDGE THROUGH COLOR library simply list the titles and mail to:

BANTAM BOOKS, INC.
Dept. KTC-1
666 Fifth Avenue
New York, N.Y. 10019

Add 25¢ to your order to cover postage and handling. Send check or money order — please! We cannot be responsible for orders containing cash.

— A Free Bantam Catalog Available Upon Request —